[Handwritten: 2002]

[Handwritten: Merry Dear Fred, from mom]

Best Fish Ever

[Handwritten: Enjoy!]

The Indispensable Guide For
All Anglers and Non-Anglers
Who Love Eating Fish

[Handwritten: + as I recall you don't - but do try now! John O, Cartier]

John O. Cartier

Published by: Cartier Associates, Inc.
Ludington, MI 49431

Best Fish Ever
The Indispensable Guide For All Anglers And Non-Anglers Who Love Eating Fish
by John O. Cartier

Copyright © 1999 by John O. Cartier
First printing 1999
Printed in the United States of America

Cover photos and design by John O. Cartier
Cover color and coordination by RuthAnn Lueck
Layout and design by Kay Richey
Electronically created camera-ready copy by
  KLR Communications, Inc.
  POB 192
  Grawn, MI 49637
Art illustrations by Ed Sutton
  White River Wildlife Art
  11873 Scott Park Rd.
  Delton, MI 49046
  231-671-4430

Best Fish Ever: The Indispensable Guide For Anglers And Non-Anglers Who Love Eating Fish / by John O. Cartier
Fish and Fish recipes - North America

ISBN   0 - 9647193 - 1 - 2

Acknowledgments

Apart from the individuals cited in this book by name, I thank the hundreds or more expert anglers, guides, outfitters, fisheries experts and chefs who contributed their bits of cooking information that made this book possible.

I want to express my particular thanks to Dave and Kay Richey for their expertise, enthusiasm and perspectives in helping me get this book into print. They are truly top experts in the field of publishing outdoor books.

Last but by no means least is Ed Sutton who provided the illustrations. They add a special appeal not found in most wildlife art.

Books by John O. Cartier

1. MODERN WATERFOWLING

2. MODERN DEER HUNTING

3. 20 GREAT TROPHY HUNTS

4. HUNTING NORTH AMERICAN WATERFOWL

5. HOW TO GET YOUR DEER

6. BEST VENISON EVER

BEST FISH EVER - $20.75 & BEST VENISON EVER - $16.75 postpaid. (Michigan residents add 6% sales tax per book.) Books can be ordered by mail. Send check or money order to:

John O. Cartier
POB 68
Ludington, MI 49431
231 843-2764

Dedication

This book is dedicated to the 40 million sport fishermen and women who love to eat the fish they don't release. It's also for the untold millions of non-anglers who have to buy fish before they can cook and enjoy it. Both groups are looking for all the help they can get in making their fish dinners the best tasting food in the world. My purpose in writing these pages is to supply that help with the most practical information available today.

Contents

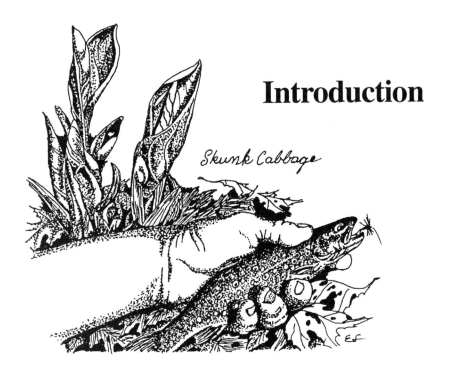

Introduction

Skunk Cabbage

This book is for the 40 million American fishermen and women who have access to the healthiest and best tasting food in the world. Many anglers catching that food have little knowledge of the best methods of preparing and cooking their fish. I'm going to tell you exactly how to do these things according to my 40 plus years of experience.

I began my outdoor writing career over 50 years ago. In those days I didn't know much about cooking, and I wasn't interested in learning many details. My desire was to become the best outdoor writer in the business.

I became good enough to be offered a full-time job with OUTDOOR LIFE magazine in 1965. As Midwest Field Editor I fished hundreds of lakes and streams from northern Alaska to Mexico, and from the east coast to the west coast of the United States. I wrote five books on hunting and fishing, and hundreds of magazine feature articles. All of my writings were published by OUTDOOR LIFE magazine and the OUTDOOR LIFE BOOK CLUB. All of my fishing articles were about catching, none about cooking.

During those years I ate hundreds of fish dinners prepared by guides, outfitters and talented anglers. Somewhere along the way I started wondering why some of those dinners were so much better than others. I began using a special notebook to record information about the best fish and game dinners I had the privilege to enjoy.

By the time I took early retirement, after I'd put in 20 years with OUTDOOR LIFE, I had a real wealth of information in that notebook. I'd also developed an obsession for properly preparing fish and game. I had more time to cook and I had more fish and game to work with. Eventually it dawned on me that I could be of great help to outdoorsmen if I wrote about the most important things I'd learned.

I began by writing a book titled BEST VENISON EVER. I chose this subject because I'd long been aware that many hunters ruin their meat long before it's cooked. A commercial meat processor would grimace and shake his head in disbelief if he watched how a lot of venison is taken care of in the field.

The situation is even worse with fish. Properly cleaned venison will improve if properly aged. Fish can't, it just gets fishier. The only way to getting the best out of a meal of fish is in the handling and preparation long before cooking. That's what much of this book will be about, and it will follow the same format that proved so successful with BEST VENISON EVER.

I published my venison cookbook late in 1995. I figured it was the last book I'd ever write, but what happened next convinced me that I should write another book titled BEST FISH EVER.

Some orders for my venison book were accompanied by notes asking if I offered similar information about cooking fish. My casual interest was intensified when many customers reordered additional copies. Here are some typical comments.

"I ordered your book for my husband's Xmas present. I liked it so much I want three more for other gifts. Have you written a book about cooking fish?" Shirley Quattro, Lake Orion, MI

"I received my copy of your book and I want to tell you it's excellent. I want 10 more copies to give to members of my outdoor club. Do you have material on the best preparation and cooking methods for fish?" Ralph Johnson, Lake Forest, IL

"I read your book cover to cover twice while recovering from surgery.

After a lifetime of hunting I thought I knew all there was to know about venison. I was wrong. Do you offer similar information on cooking fish?" Frank Potkey, Drunns, PA

After I read comments like those enough times I decided I could probably do a lot of fishermen a lot of good if I got this old typewriter humming one more time. But I made one decision right away. I wanted the book to emphasize that there is no way anybody can cook a great fish dinner by using inferior quality fish. So this book is far less a cookbook than the typical volume loaded with recipes. It's an attempt to offer the much needed advice on how to handle your fish from the time you catch them until the time you eat them.

Americans are becoming more hooked on fish every year. Its popularity began as a low-fat alternative to red meat and a stand-in for poultry. For two decades, beef has been losing market share in retail outlets. Its share of the retail consumer's dollar has fallen dramatically. In 1980, 61.5% of what shoppers spent on meat went for beef. By 1996 that figure had tumbled to 46.5%.

A lot of those lost dollars are now being spent on fish. That's a huge advantage for the sport fisherman. As the public demand for more fish increased, the seafood industry responded with more research on fish care and cooking. Once consumers began sampling todays' lighter, simpler fish dishes -- in place of the breaded deep-fried entrees of old-- they realized that not all fish tastes the same. Now we have scientific proof that the best ways to cook fish are also the easiest. I'll cover all the important details in the following chapters. But I want to emphasize here that never before in history has the sport angler had such great opportunities to enjoy the very best meals from the fish he catches.

I'll mention an anecdote that proves the point. It involved a doctor friend. As far as I know he never had a bad experience with eating fish, he just preferred other food. That happens to a lot of people who eat fish in ordinary less expensive restaurants. They just never had the opportunity to experience the enormous difference in quality between wholesale commercial and fresh-caught fish. The northern pike pieces I sauteed that night never even made it to dining room table before the good doctor got into them. He soon discovered the enormous gourmet feast he had been missing all his life.

It was winter. My son and I had caught the pike on tipups that afternoon. I had filleted them so they were bone free. I was frying fish on the workbench in our garage. The wood stove was going full blast. It was warm and comfortable in there even though the outside temperature was zero.

I had a big platter covered with several layers of paper toweling. As my fillet pieces finished cooking I'd remove them from the pan and put them on the paper toweling to absorb what little grease was left. Doctor Jim saw me doing this, and walked over to get a sample. His whole body seemed to relax as he ate the first piece of fillet. Then he tried another. After that he just stood there, completely absorbed with eating fish. I think he forgot he was at a party, and that maybe he shouldn't be eating all those fillets before anybody else had a chance at them. Finally he turned to me and said, "Your pike, without question, is by far the best fish I've ever eaten!"

Preparing and cooking fish correctly involves far more than simply making a meal. Fish can be prepared, cooked and presented in so many ways that it's always possible to bring out flavors that will surely please any appetite. You have to know who you're cooking for because taste preferences vary tremendously. A friend, who fishes almost exclusively for Lake Michigan salmon, puts it well when he says, "There must be 100 ways to cook salmon. I personally prefer to grill king-salmon steaks cut 1-inch thick. My folks think oven-broiled fillets are much better. A fishing buddy's family thinks everybody misses super meals by not poaching salmon. If you cook enough fish you'll get to know what you and your guests prefer.

These thoughts emphasize that fish is not just something to eat anymore. Great fish has become something to be entertained by. It's the perfect central theme for gatherings of friends, especially if you catch your own fish. My favorite way of entertaining is to take a couple of friends angling for a few hours. Then I fillet our catch and cook it fresh. The wives show up for dinner and everybody has a wonderful time. It's the best and cheapest way to go for great entertainment.

Culinary experts credit the boom in television chefs--beginning in the early 1990's--with making the cooking of fish both easy and appealing. It was the greatest thing to happen because it started demistifying the whole

11

chef trade. Anglers who didn't keep many fish because they didn't know the best ways of cleaning and cooking them began seeing chefs on outdoor programs showing how to get the job done.

About the same time came the news that fish is the ultimate health food. Several scientific studies determined that eating fish provides many health benefits that we can get from no other source. But this is true only if you know how to care for your fish after you catch them. I'll get into the health benefits in chapter two. Suffice it to say here that mounting medical evidence suggests that people who eat fish at least once a week tend to live healthier and longer lives. When we combine that knowledge with the long-known fact that fishing is emotionally therapeutic, we just about eliminate any excuse not to go fishing.

There is one last major reason why sport fishing has boomed in popularity while participation in hunting activities continues to decrease. The key word is access. The situation in my home state of Michigan proves the point dramatically.

Some fishing in Michigan now is far superior to what it ever was in the so-called "good old days." Fifty years ago there wasn't a single salmon in Lake Michigan. Today there are millions of them, and hundreds of thousands of sport anglers get the fishing thrills of their lifetimes by catching them. They can fish any place they want to on the big lake. All that water out there is free as long as you purchase a fishing license and salmon/trout stamp for Michigan waters.

The same thing is true for boat anglers on the state's inland lakes and most rivers and streams. Also, many of those waters have benefited from aggressive stocking programs. The lake I live on has a great walleye fishery, a situation that didn't exist only a few years ago. Anybody who has a fishing license can go after those walleyes, and they can fish any part of the lake without having to get permission from anybody.

Compare that magnificent situation with what has happened to hunting. Michigan used to have great pheasant hunting. It's gone now, destroyed by modern farming practices and a huge increase in predators. The two really bright spots left are goose and whitetail deer hunting, and those activities are being hit harder and harder with the growing access problem. Most of the geese and deer are on private land, and more and more landowners are turning to leasing hunting rights for big money. You can get great hunting if you want to pay, but you can get excellent fishing on nearby public waters without paying anything for access.

And there are two last huge advantages for anglers. Some fishing seasons are open all year, and all others usually last much longer than hunting seasons. Finally, no fisherman ever has to cut away bullet-damaged meat.

Once your fish are caught and cleaned the goal is to find recipes that enhance flavor and texture while maximizing nutritional advantages. Cooking fish is relatively easy, but I've tried to simplify, streamline and uncomplicate each recipe in this book so any cook can use them. Fish dishes are appropriate for any occasion and in all seasons.

You should also know that many types of fish are interchangeable. Salt water fish have different flavors than freshwater species, but methods of cooking are often identical. One key factor is size of the pieces of fish you're going to cook. A walleye fillet, for example, may be about the same size as a fillet from a red snapper. Your favorite cooking method will work equally well with both species.

My fishing experiences have been mostly with freshwater species, but my fish-eating experiences have involved many species of the ocean's bounty. Regardless of where the fish comes from, always use cooking methods appropriate to the size of fish pieces you're working with. I emphasize this important rule because it's something I forgot to do in my venison cookbook. It caused unnecessary trouble for many readers. The following is part of one of many letters I received on the subject.

"I've lived in Alaska for 35 years, but still get game and fish news from North Dakota. I read about your book, and am wondering if I can use some of your venison recipes with moose and caribou meat. Our deep freeze is full of this stuff, and my wife would like to try various ways of cooking it." John M. Webster, Anchorage, AK

The answer, of course, is absolutely yes. All big game and all species of fish lend themselves to similar recipes, as long as you work with similar cuts of meat. With game you use different cooking methods for roasts than you would for steaks. With fish the main difference is whether the flesh is fat and oily or lean and dry meated.

Some examples of oily meated freshwater fish include trout, salmon and whitefish. These species are subject to specific cooking methods. Broiling and grilling always works best with oily-meated fish. (See chart page 62.)

Lean or dry-meated fish are best suited for deep frying or sauteing. Popular freshwater species include perch, northern pike, bluegills and walleye. Some of their ocean counterparts are red snapper, cod, haddock, halibut and flounder.

In many places throughout this book I write about the benefits of catch-and-release fishing and the advantages of modern fish-management programs. But there are still some waters where natural fish production is so prolific that overfishing may never happen. Florida's lake Okeechobee is a top example.

This huge lake, 467,200 surface acres, is so fertile it annually yields over 1 million crappies to anglers. Local fishermen catch so many bass and crappies during winter months they seldom bother with the fantastic bluegill fishing that peaks in April and May. That's when hordes of visiting anglers regularly fill the motels and other rental units. One marina sends 500 to 600 pounds of cleaned bluegill carcasses to the dump each DAY. Game and Fresh Water Fish Commission biologist Tim Coughlin claims that such huge harvests are probably the best means for keeping the lake's fish populations in balance and preventing stunting. Big O's whopper bluegills are so abundant they support Florida's only commerical freshwater fishery.

When I first heard about such amazing angler success I wondered if it could really be true. I called Clewiston based Danny Watkins, who is an Orvis-endorsed fly-fishing guide. "Yes" he said. "It's all gospel." Phone him at 800 741-2517

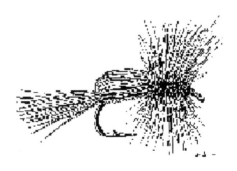

Truly
Great
Eating

Even though the current craze to eat fish is reaching ever new heights, it's still amazing that 90 percent of Americans have never...ever...enjoyed a truly great fish dinner. This is because the opportunity to get really fresh fish has been hard to come by. Up until recent years the average American simply didn't have access to truly fresh fish. Only the sport fisherman enjoyed this unique opportunity.

According to studies made by Texas A & M University, seafood still accounts for only 14 percent of total meat consumption in the United States. That's up from eight percent 10 years ago, but it ties in with a 1998 study by the National Cattlemen's Beef Association. This study reports that annual per capita meat consumption has decreased by 15 pounds since 1980. Clearly, more people are eating more fish, but most still aren't getting truly great eating.

Probably a minimum of at least half of all sport fishermen have no more than a basic understanding of how fish must be cared for to make excellent table fare. Many fishermen simply don't realize that correct and complete care of the catch is a complicated art that is difficult to master. The really best fish dinners are prepared by those few anglers who realize that a fishing trip isn't over until the catch is properly cleaned and cooked.

Those of us who enjoy cleaning, cooking and freezing fish are the only ones who can appreciate the taste and flavors of truly great fish year around. How can you enjoy cleaning fish? Part of it is the satisfaction of doing the job in the best possible manner consistent with quality, but some statistics will help brighten the picture.

Pound for pound, fish is higher in protein and lower in calories than beef, pork or lamb. Fish is low in saturated fats and cholesterol, high in vitamins A and D, and low in sodium. It's easily digested, is naturally tender, has no bones if properly filleted, and requires minimum cooking times.

The angler who catches his own fish has access to the freshest product. Even his frozen fish can be far superior to that purchased in markets. He may smoke, can or pickle far more recipes than are available in stores; and he has access to numerous species not sold commercially.

Knowing all this boils down to the standard response I offer anybody who asks me: "How can you prepare such delicious fish?"

"I discovered long ago," I tell them, "that the only way to eat great fish is to know exactly how to take care of them. If you know how it's done and you do it yourself you have total control."

If there's a key word to the entire process it has to be RELAX. You must have enough time to do the job correctly. The secret to everything is knowing why fish spoil so rapidly.

While healthy fish flesh itself is bacteria free, bacteria abound on the surface of the fish and in the digestive tract. Once the fish dies after being caught the flesh becomes vulnerable to these micro-organisms. The process progresses rapidly, especially when the weather is hot and the water is warm. this is when gastric juices eat through stomach-wall linings almost immediately.

Just as important is the physiology involved. Fish, like animals and humans, store glycogen (animal starch) in their tissues. However, the energy expended when fish are struggling to get free after being hooked uses up that stockpiled glycogen, so none remains to act as a preservative after the fish dies. Finally, the highly unsaturated fat of fish can easily take up extra oxygen, and that leads to rancidity and rapid spoilage.

The best way to keep a fish from spoiling is to keep it alive until you clean it. No deterioration can begin until the fish dies. Anglers having boats equipped with aerated live wells have the best bets. A submerged wire fish basket works well. If fish can't be kept alive they should be killed immediately after catching, then placed into a cooler with a layer of crushed ice. Tests have shown that fish keep much longer when placed on crushed ice than on ice cubes or bags of ice.

The worst thing to do is throw freshly caught fish into a bucket of water or non-iced fish box. Here they go through the stress of slowly dying. Within minutes they begin to spoil rapidly, completely eliminating any chance of becoming ingredients for a great fish dinner. Putting fish on a stringer is at least as bad. In this case they slowly drown and begin spoiling long before the unknowing angler suspects trouble.

With some important exceptions, most fish are not really cleaned until they are reduced to boneless and skinless fillets. When you eliminate the bones and skin you're discarding parts that can produce the fishy and/or muddy tastes that so many anglers put up with in their fish dinners. Some of the notable exceptions are small stream trout, yellow perch, small to medium-size walleyes; and steaks cut from salmon, steelhead, lake trout and several ocean species.

One of the best gourmet fish-eating experiences comes with lunch on a flat bank near the stream that produced some small trout only hours ago. These little beauties, gilled and gutted and fried long enough to crisp the skin, are about as tasty as fish can get.

The same thinking applies to lake perch and small walleyes taken from cold, clean water. The taste of the skin, sauteed crisp, is a delicacy in itself. That is why ... when you buy lake perch and most walleye fillets in quality seafood markets ... you get them with the skin intact. I'm aware that some cooks rave about baked whole fish, often with unscaled skins and heads still attached and bodies stuffed with dressing. Such dramatic presentations are not for me. I usually want to cook pieces of 100 percent meat.

The cooking of fish is far less complicated than the cleaning. The basic elements are very simple. Go with the rule that you'll always do best if you never under estimate the power of simplicity. I'll tell you how important this principle is with some of the greatest chefs I've ever met.

Le Cirque 2000 was rated the best restaurant of the year by Esquire magazine. This establishment had a price tag of $6 million in 1997 when it opened on Madison Avenue in New York. It employs 27 cooks who must prepare everything perfectly for the celebrity clientele that doesn't mind paying $63 to well over $100 for a three-course dinner.

Would you like to try head Chef's Sottha Khunn's duck? You can get the breast cooked slightly pink with parchment-crisp skin. The legs come braised in Eastern curries, taro and lotus root. Would you prefer venison? A partial saddle of it comes with foie gras, braised in Bordeaux, then served with a puree of autumn's sweetest chestnuts.

So what kind of exotic preparation does Khunn use for fish? Working out of the $3 million kitchen he often does practically nothing. "If I can get flown-in fish at its freshest I refuse to ruin its flavor," he says without a bit of pretense. "I'll likely do nothing more than saute the fillets quickly and serve them forthwith!"

That comes from a man who can cook everything imaginable in a restaurant. A similar viewpoint is found in Dallas at a restaurant called simply FISH. This place doesn't have a million-dollar design. It takes a straightforward approach to cooking a wide variety of seafood in the best possible ways. Chef Christian Svalesen is not about to bury the natural flavor of fish under syrupy reductions or overly rich toppings.

"I don't use many sauces either," he says. "The few I do use are light with appropriate flavors that go well with fish. I strongly believe in leaving good fish pretty much alone."

If the world's best cooks believe that simple and easy cooking is the way to go, so should we. In the entire canon of fish cookery, nothing can surpass the juiciness and crispness of simplicity.

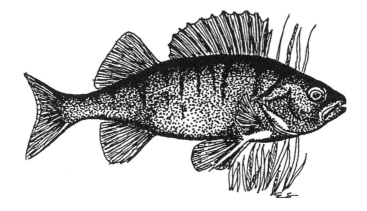

Fish Is The Ultimate Health Food

Almost every health-conscious person knows by now that fish is good for you. And yes, fish really is brain food; that's also been proven in recent years. So not only is fish a delicacy to savor, but it's one of healthiest choices for dinner at least once a week. What most of us don't know is why all this is true. The best way to find out is to get the opinions of experts.

One of the top professionals in the field is Sonja Conner, a registered dietitian and co-author of the "New American Diet." The book was co-written with her husband, Dr. William Conner. He is an acknowledge leader in fish oil research at the University of Oregon Health Sciences Center.

"One major effect that eating fish has on LDL cholesterol has nothing to do with the much publicized omega-3 oils," says Dr. Connor. "The key knowledge is that fish is simply low in fat. Most of the red meat people eat (hamburger, roasts, steaks, etc.) is 25 to 30 percent fat. But the range of fat in fish is closer to one percent, almost never higher than 12 percent. Also, a significant amount of the fat in meat is saturated. That greasy stuff, with the cholesterol we eat, does the most to increase bad LDL cholesterol. The small amount of fat in fish is largely polyunsaturated, which lowers LDL. These simple facts in themselves should be enough to convince people to eat lots of fish!"

Sonja Connor points out that fat calories in fish can be driven up and made saturated by deep frying in oil or broiling in butter. These are the two most common methods of preparation in less expensive restaurants. The better restaurants will cook fish any way the customer wants it. Fish can easily be prepared without added fats by baking, grilling, sauteing, steaming, poaching, braising or broiling with butter substitutes. That's great information to utilize when cooking fish you catch.

Now let's clear up the confusion about the omega-3 fatty oils found in fish. They have been rightly touted by medical experts as the agents responsible for a variety of heart-associated health benefits. These fats also have protective benefits against cancer and inflammatory conditions. The most significant factor about them is that they occur only in fish and marine animals. If you eat a lot of fish or other seafood you get these enormous health benefits for free. Tell that to your wife the next time she says you're spending too much time fishing.

Omega-3 is only part of the picture. Fish is also an excellent source of protein, it's low in calories, high in polyunsaturated fat (the good kind), low in salt, and a great source of vitamins and minerals.

An average 4-ounce serving of fish provides over 20 grams of complete protein. That's about half the protein we need each day. Most fish also contains less than 100 calories in that 4-ounce serving. Compare that with 160 calories for a similar portion of chicken, and more than 200 calories for beef.

One of the most recent research articles on the benefits of eating fish adds even more scientific evidence to this overall health message. A group of researchers in Seattle, lead by Dr. David Siscovik, discovered that fish consumption was associated with 50 percent reduction in the risk of cardiac arrest. It was further determined that only one high-fat fish meal, or two medium-fat fish meals per week produced this benefit.

High-fat fish include such species as salmon, lake trout and whitefish. One 4-ounce serving of high-fat fish contains about 300 calories. A similar size serving of low-fat fish contains only about 125 calories.

All of this knowledge has been a long time coming, but it was accelerated by the relatively recent health craze. What really opened the eyes of nutrition experts was news that Greenland Eskimos were practically immune to heart disease, despite diets lacking fiber, vitamins C and

E and being overloaded with fat ... all known causes of heart trouble. The natives eat huge amounts of cholesterol-rich whale blubber, fatty fish and seal, but have the healthiest hearts in the world.

Researchers at first believed that Greenland Eskimos have a "genetic protection" against heart disease. This was recognized as a mistake and clearly disproved when some of these Eskimos adopted a standard Western diet. Within a few years their rate of heart disease rose to equal the average American rate. Those that went back to their native fish diets had a dramatic drop in heart disease. The benefit of eating more fish is undeniable.

Almost every major health organization now recommends getting omega-3 fatty acids from eating fish instead of taking fish-oil supplements. Some of these organizations include the NATIONAL INSTITUTE OF HEALTH, the AMERICAN HEART ASSOCIATION, the NATIONAL CANCER INSTITUTE, the AMERICAN MEDICAL ASSOCIATION and many more.

There has never been a better time to eat fish, and it will get even better if you follow the tips and suggestions in the rest of this book.

Bits and Pieces of Helpful Information

Here are some tips and tidbits of information that will help fine-tune your cooking of fish. Keep these gems in mind while reading the following chapters.

The most recent Fishing Motivation Study prepared for the AMERI-CAN SPORTFISHING ASSOCIATION showed that over 80 percent of fishing in America is in freshwater. It also showed that Americans spent $104 billion on wildlife-related recreation during the study year. That compares with $81 billion spent on new cars during the same period. That's astounding, and it proves that there is an enormous amount of fish taken home for dinner!

What do all these fresh-water anglers fish for most? Here's the breakdown:

Bass	35 %
Trout	18 %
Catfish	11 %
All species	9 %

Bluegills or bream.......... 6 %
Crappie........................... 6 %
Walleye.......................... 5 %
Striper........................... 5 %
Perch ....3 %
Salmon........................... 2 %

Although bass are by far the most popular quarry to catch they are way down the list of best eating species. This book is designed to help you cook the best possible fish dinners with little emphasis on species. You will find bass recipes in the following pages, but mostly you'll find the techniques for properly preparing and cooking all species of edible fish.

Many anglers don't realize how delicate and perishable fish are. High-quality fish should be cleaned and cooked, frozen or continually iced as soon as possible after the catch. Most refrigerators hold a temperature of about 40 degrees F. This is not cold enough to retain top quality. It's a fact that fish held at 32 degrees keeps twice as well as those held at 42 degrees. Fish held in a hot car can spoil in 30 minutes. Forever remember that the quality of your fish dinner depends on maintaining fresh-caught freshness right up to cooking time.

There are several tricks to keeping fish as cold as possible in a refrigerator. The bottom of a refrig is colder than the top. The bottom will be even colder if the temperature control is moved to its coldest setting. You can also fill a bottom vegetable bin with crushed ice, thus making the coldest part still colder. Fillets wrapped in plastic wrap and covered with crushed ice will retain top quality for 4 days.

Quality of fish kept in crushed ice begins to deteriorate after 5 days. Freezing a good piece of fish the day it's caught will make a far better meal in 6 days than if you kept the same fillet iced for the same length of time.

Cooking fish is like cooking anything else regarding tastes. You can't please everyone so it's best to please yourself. If you like medium to well-done fish go with thin cuts at high temperature. Thicker cuts cooked the same length of time at high temperature are best for those who prefer their fish with barely-cooked centers. If you prefer a thicker cut cooked medium or well done, go with a medium cooking temperature for a longer period of time to enable the heat to penetrate the fillet. In a nutshell, that's all there is to cooking fish.

Recently I came across a magnificent coffee-table book on fishing. It's 429 pages contain great information on species history, types of tackle, how-to-catch techniques and most everything else about how to go fishing. The huge book is loaded with beautiful color photos and lots of charts and graphs that further explain how to catch fish. But there is not a single sentence on cleaning and cooking the catch, the one subject many anglers value the most.

It's always a good idea to rinse fish quickly under cold, running water before beginning your cooking preparations. This will reduce surface bacteria and improve taste whether your fillets are fresh cleaned or defrosted. No matter what you do with fish, bacteria collects first on the surface where it's easiest to wash away.

There is no easier way to ruin great fish than to fry it in old cooking oil that needed to be changed. Don't use oil or grease more than once for cooking fish.

Intestinal tracts of all fish are loaded with blood, slime and digestive juices that will taint meat almost immediately when accidently punctured. Beginners at filleting are especially guilty of cutting into this tract and releasing enzymes before they realize what they've done. If your knife slips, quickly rinse and clean the affected area. Better yet, until you become an expert, consider gutting your fish before filleting.

From a nutritional standpoint, fish are categorized as high fat or low fat. High-fat fish such as salmon have over 12 grams of fat per 4-ounce serving. Low fat species such as pike and perch, have about 1-1/2 grams per 4-ounce serving. In general, saltwater fish contain more fatty oils than freshwater fish. The healthiest fish you can eat are freshwater panfish that live in cold-water steams and lakes and are caught when they're just big enough to fillet.

Preparing good fish dishes requires some planning just like any other kind of cooking. But in no other meal preparations do ultra-fresh ingredients in proper amounts play such an important part. Attention to cooking techniques are rather basic. The resulting meals keep getting better and better with the experience of repetition. Pick out the recipes in this book that appeal to you, then work with them a few times. It won't take many repetitions of the same cooking experience before you're putting top-quality fish dinners on the table every time. You can't do that with the complicated recipes you'll find in most cookbooks. BEST FISH EVER keeps things simple.

If you cut your fillets into three-inch-wide chunks, you can cook or freeze meal-size portions that are all approximately the same thickness. This means that all pieces will get done at the same time in the cooking process. Use another trick if your three-inch pieces vary in thickness. If I'm sauteing, I cook all the thickest pieces together in the first batch. The thinner pieces go into the pan for the second session. When cooking a single batch, simply remove the thinnest pieces first.

Since all fried or sauted fish are usually coated with some type of seasoned flour it's wise to use a top quality product that best suits your appetite. If you cook with a poor-grade mix you'll be losing flavor and texture. Experiment until you find the flour that best suits your taste. The same is true with cooking oil or grease.

All through this book I talk about using crushed ice for cooling fish. It does a much better job than cubes or blocks. The idea is to get the ice into contact with as much fish surface as possible. Crushed or shaved ice will mold to fish or fillet forms, cubes or blocks can't do this. If you're cooling dressed fish be sure to pack ice inside the body cavity and all around the fish. And always make sure there's plenty of ice below the fish flesh and the bottom of the cooler. If the flesh soaks in ice melt it will spoil in a hurry. That's why it's important to use a cooler with a drain.

Some folk's lack of enthusiasm for fish can be traced to the "fishy" odor that may permeate the kitchen after cooking fish. There are two things to know about this situation. First, truly fresh fish does not smell "fishy" either before or after cooking unless it's fried. Two, if you stay away from frying and wash your utensils with soapy water soon after using them you should have no problem with unwanted smells. If you insist on deep-frying, you'll need little more than the moist inside of half a lemon to eliminate the smell. Cut the pulpy rind open to form a flat piece. Use it as a wipe on both your hands and your cutting surfaces after cooking. Then spray a citrus-flavored room deodorizer to finish the job.

Another great solution to the fried fish problem is the "Friday Fish Fry" that's so welcome in Heartland states. Whether the main course is perch, walleye, cod or catfish the Friday night fries remain a tradition where diners appreciate the camaraderie as much as the great eating. Whether the 'fry' is held at a tavern, supper club or community club or hall, the smell of hot oil and sizzling fish fills the rooms.

At the best fish fries you'll wait an hour or more to get served because these meals are extremely popular. How popular? At Milwaukee's Serb Memorial Hall huge fish fries have taken place every Friday for more than 30 years. On a recent Good Friday the hall served 4,522 people who downed 2-1/4 tons of fish with 80 gallons of tartar sauce and a small mountain of coleslaw. So, obviously, there's an enormous number of people who love the smell and taste of deep-fried fish.

Here's the scoop on the fat (oil content) of fish. The amount of food available to each species appears to be the major controlling factor. Water with a prolific forage base yield fish with the most fat. Fish caught in winter have less fat because they don't eat as much. The oil content of various species may vary by more than 200 times, and intraspecies variation may be as high as 10 times.

Of most significance to the angler is the fact that the fat content of any fish increases from least at the tail section to most in the forward part of the body. Steaks cut near the head may have as much as 80 percent more oil than tail-end-cuts. Also, the belly and flesh along the lateral line (where the meat is always darker) are always fattier. So, when you fillet a fish, remember that the tail sections have the least fat and are boneless, making them the choicest cuts you can eat.

The best fish dinners appeal to three vital senses: sight, smell and taste. Sight is the most important with white-meat fish because they are dull to look at. People form hard opinions about a meal long before they actually taste it. It's best to dress up lean fillets with a garnishing of color.

Start with chopped herbs like chives, parsley or oregano. Sprinkle them over the cooked white flesh. All citrus makes a natural compliment with fish, so edge the fillet with a few wedges of orange or lemon. You can add color before cooking by sprinkling each fillet with paprika.

If you want to saute or grill fish before guests arrive, slightly undercook it. Line an oven-proof platter with two layers of paper toweling. Spread the meat on the toweling. Cover with another layer of toweling. If there's plenty of time before dinner set oven control to warm. If the meal is to be served within an hour set oven control to 150 degrees. Either way the fish will finish firming up while the toweling absorbs excess cooking oil.

Ever wonder why fried or sauted fish has maximum taste appeal right after it's cooked, but leftovers are lousy for lunch the next day? I have a solution that works great for me.

During the original cooking the hot oil stays sizzling on the outside of the fish but doesn't penetrate the meat. After dinner and overnight, when the flesh cools, the residual cooking oil does penetrates the meat. So when you reheat leftovers the next day you're heating oil that has soaked into the meat, thereby creating an oily taste.

One day some years ago I reasoned that if I didn't cook potential leftovers in oil or grease there couldn't be any remaining bad taste. So when I finished sauteing enough for dinner I loosely wiped out the pan with toweling. Then I cooked the remaining fillets in normal fashion...minus all oil except a thin film remaining in the pan. Much to my surprise they tasted pretty good the next day. Not as good as fresh cooked, but definitely much better than the usual leftovers. The crisp, golden outside appearance of the meat was missing, but an excellent taste was still there because there was no absorbed oil to destroy it.

Here are two items that really help when grilling lean fish prone to sticking on hot grates. A skewer rack rests fish kebabs just above the grate where they can't possibly stick. A hinged grilling basket does the same job when cooking fish pieces, fillets, or even small trout.

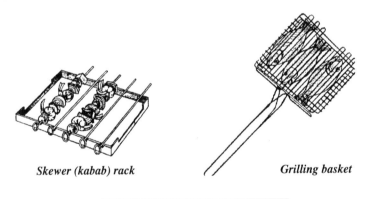

Skewer (kabab) rack   *Grilling basket*

Microwaving fish plays no role in this book. My experiments with trying to cook fish this way have been disasters. There is nothing as unpalatable as overcooked microwaved fish. Why do I feel so strongly?

First off, the main benefit of the microwave is speed. Why does any cook need speed with fish that cooks so fast anyway? Then there's the fact that microwaves don't cook evenly, resulting in fish that are cooked rare on one side and overdone on the other unless you have mastered instant control. You don't need instant control? Well, consider that a 6-ounce fish fillet will cook in under a minute in some microwave ovens. I can't work with that type of cooking.

But there are great new developments coming fast. A revolutionary oven that cooks with the speed of a microwave and the quality of a regular oven has already been developed for restaurant use. Two manufactures claimed in April 1999 that a residential version of this oven will be on the market in 2000. The cooking technology combines high-powered micro-waves that cook the food from inside out, with 60-mile-per-hour hot air blasts that crisp the food from the outside in. A shroud around the food ensures even cooking.

I don't recommend steaming as a way of cooking fish either. You can buy fish-steaming equipment for about $30, or you can make do with any pot that has a tight-fitting lid plus an oiled rack to hold fish pieces above gently boiling liquid. The liquid may or may not be flavored. The important thing is that steaming doesn't produce the uniform cooking results of poaching or braising, particularly braising which is the best of the three methods for adding flavor. (See chapter 6 for all the details.)

One of the biggest mistakes home cooks make is stinting on knives. If you can't slice and chop with ease, cooking fish becomes unnecessarily frustrating. The best knives are expensive, but worth every penny if you cook a lot of fish and vegetable side dishes. Use knives with blades made of high-carbon stain-resistant steel that can be easily sharpened again and again. Cheap stainless steel knives can't be sharpened well once they become dull or damaged, especially filleting knives. Get a good one, keep it sharp, and use it only for cleaning fish and nothing else.

Your filleting and kitchen knives should have comfortable grips. Once you handle knives in a good kitchen-equipment store you'll know which ones feel best for you. A comfortable knife of top quality gives you the pleasure of complete cutting control with less cutting effort.

Fillet knife

Ever hear of fish hash? Here's a recipe that works great for any lean-fish fillet cut into 1-inch pieces. It's wonderful with eggs for breakfast, seasoned bread for lunch, or on its own for a midnight snack. Use 4 medium-size fillets. Serves 4.

>3 tablespoons cooking oil
>8 new medium potatoes sliced thin and diced
>2 small red or green bell peppers, diced
>1 large onion, diced, mixed with
>1 thinly sliced garlic clove
>2 fresh tomatoes, peeled and diced
>2 tablespoons chopped parsley and chives

In 12-inch skillet cook potatoes over medium heat until tender and beginning to brown. Add peppers, garlic and onion and continue sauteing about 5 minutes. Add pieces and cook 5 minutes more, stirring occasionally. Add tomatoes and seasoning to taste. Saute and stir 2 more minutes. That's all there is to it.

Salt-free cooking is never bland when you add zest with herbs and spices. Just remember that dried herbs are stronger than fresh, and powdered are stronger than crushed. A useful formula is: 1/4 teaspoon powered = 1 teaspoon crumbled = 2 teaspoons fresh.

For stovetop sauteing, be sure to use a heavy high-side skillet or electric frying pan with a good quality nonstick surface. Such a pan holds even cooking temperatures and minimizes the need for added fat. The best width for general fish cooking is 12 inches. Get a tight-fitting cover for spatter control. The next best accessory is a slotted nonstick medium-wide spatula. These tools are all you need for all the sauteing, deep-frying, poaching and braising you'll want to do.

When grilling fillets without a grill basket lay them perpendicular to grate bars. This ensures minimum contact of fish flesh with hot metals, which helps prevent sticking.

It is not dangerous to refreeze thawed fish as long as it was fresh when it was originally frozen, was properly thawed, and is not refrigerated for more than 1 1/2 days. The goal is to keep this fish continually cold until it's cooked or refrozen. Remember though, that refreezing diminishes taste quality.

Of all the freshwater fish species most suitable for freezing, salmon ranks near the bottom of the list. Of all fishes worldwide most suitable for canning, salmon ranks near the top of the list. That's why canning serves salmon fishermen much better than freezing. Canned salmon can be eaten 2 or 3 years after being preserved without loss of taste quality. And you can make a great spread out of it. Try this recipe:

1 pint chopped canned salmon
1/4 cup chopped green onion
1 8-ounce package softened cream cheese
1 tablespoon lemon juice
2 tablespoons chopped parsley

Blend all ingredients except parsley. Keep refrigerated until serving time. Spread on cocktail crackers, sprinkling parsley on top. Makes 1 1/2 cups salmon spread.

The butter served with seafood in better restaurants is clarified butter. It's the only butter you should use for sauteing at high temperatures because it does not spatter or burn as easily as unclarified butter. Make 2 cups this way:

In a medium skillet, slowly melt 1 pound of regular butter over low heat. Skim off the surfaxce foam, then pour the clear yellow liquid into a bowl. Leave the milk solids that have sunk to the bottom of the skillet. Once clarified, this butter may be kept for several weeks in a bowl covered with plastic wrap.

Must Know Basics

During my 55 years of fishing I've talked with thousands of anglers. Many of those conversations sparked questions about processing and cooking fish. Here are the most frequently asked questions ... and the answers that should do you the most good.

Q. WHAT PROCESSING AND COOKING TECHNIQUE WILL GIVE ME THE BEST POSSIBLE FISH DINNER?

A. Your fish can never taste better than when cleaned and cooked near the water it recently inhabited. That's why the famous wilderness shore lunches are so good. A fish that is freshly caught, cleaned and fried or grilled in the outdoors has reached its maximum potential for superb eating.

But why wait for a wilderness trip to enjoy this gourmet pleasure? Lots of anglers now create their shore lunches close to home on waters they have fished hundreds of times. Just take along a fillet knife, a frying pan, some cooking oil, a brown bag holding a little flour laced with salt and pepper, a spatula, a small propane stove and some paper toweling. A small wooden filleting board is handy. A few slices of bread and a beverage completes the ingredients, all of which fit nicely into a pack basket. A shore lunch adds tremendous appeal to an otherwise routine day of angling.

Q. MY DIET DOESN'T INCLUDE FRIED FOODS. ARE

THERE OTHER COOKING METHODS THAT CAN BE USED FOR SHORE LUNCHES?

A. Absolutely. You can poach fish in a frying pan partly filled with boiling water. All sorts of fish meals can be steamed in foil. In fact, steaming gives the opportunity to include other ingredients. Take along a large piece of heavy-duty aluminum foil. Oil the foil before placing fillets on it so they won't stick. Add slices of onion, celery, and potato. All are items that are easy to pack and prepare. Close and seal the foil securely. Grill the package over an open fire or poach it in boiling water. Ten minutes of cooking will give you a superb meal with a minimum of fuss. A can of baked beans heated in the fire adds a great finishing touch.

Q. WHAT CAUSES CLEANED FISH TO DETERIORATE SO QUICKLY?

A. Air and water are the culprits in stealing flavor and freshness from your fillets. If you can't eat your fish the same day it is caught, and you're a day or two away from home, you should seal the meat. Enclose the fillets in Ziploc-type bags, submerge the bags in water up to the seal -- this squeezes out all the air --- then pinch the seal tight. Now place the bags between layers of crushed ice in a cooler. If you're home, and you want to keep the fish fresh for a couple of days, seal them air tight in plastic cling wrap and refrigerate.

Never let the bare meat become covered with water from melted ice. It's a sure route to quick spoilage. I'll never forget an experience showing how rapidly this can happen.

I had guests for early-spring perch fishing. This is a hit-or-miss situation. You can fill a bucket with just-spawned perch if you hit the run perfectly. If you guess wrong by only a day or two you get skunked. We got skunked. My guests badly wanted perch fillets to take home.

They saw an ad in the local paper announcing a big sale on lake perch beginning at 7 a.m. the next morning at a supermarket. We were there when the doors opened. The perch weren't displayed yet, so a clerk went to get them. He returned with a waterproof shipping container that he cut open. Inside were partially-melted ice chunks. Scores of butterflied perch fillets sloshed around in the ice and water. The meat was already beginning to turn off-color white. We looked at each other and turned to leave.

"You don't want any?" the surprised clerk asked. "They're fresh perch, we just got 'em in last night."

I wonder what those fillets tasted like when unknowing customers cooked them during the next few days. Some no doubt figured they had screwed up the cooking process. Others probably reaffirmed their convictions that they just don't like fish. None likely realized that they had cooked perch that were well into the spoilage stage, never dreaming that cleaned fish begins deteriorating almost immediately when left in standing water.

Q. I'VE USED SEVERAL METHODS FOR COOKING FISH, BUT THE FLESH ALWAYS SEEMS TO TURN OUT TOO DRY. SHOULD I BE USING SOME KIND OF SAUCE TO KEEP THE MEAT MOIST?

A. No. The odds are high that you're cooking your catch too long and at too low a temperature. Slow, prolonged cooking dries out all species of fish. Go with the 10-minute ... 350 degree rule. That translates into cooking your fish 10 minutes per inch of thickness at 350 degrees. High temperature sears the outside of the flesh, thereby preventing it from absorbing cooking oil. Grilling is a different story because the meat is farther from the heat source than in sauteing. Grilling times are normally 10 to 20 minutes over medium heat. I'll get into all the details in chapter 6.

Q. WHY IS IT THAT FISH CAUGHT IN A GIVEN LAKE OFTEN TASTE FAR BETTER THAN THE SAME SPECIES TAKEN FROM ANOTHER LAKE?

A. One of the fascinating things about the taste of fresh fish is how closely it's related to the waters it inhabits. The tastiest freshwater fish taken from cool, clean waters are always infinitely superior to those caught in warmer, more stagnate waters. Spring or stream-fed lakes can be depended on to produce great fish dinners. General rule for freshwater fish... the cooler the water the tastier the fish. That's why fish caught through the ice make better eating than the same species taken from the same lake during summer.

After you have fished enough waters enough times you'll learn where the tastiest species come from. Those are the places to go when you want fish for dinner, but they're not necessarily the waters where you'll find the fastest action. Most serious anglers today have favorite fishing holes where they release everything they catch. Catch-and-release are great programs and certainly help to maintain wonderful fisheries, but they may not be the places to go for eating fish.

One of my first fly-in trips to a wilderness lake in Ontario proved this truism in dramatic fashion. The lake where we set up camp was full of northern pike. While we were rigging tackle our Indian guide said, "Lots of big fish here, but no good for eating. Too muddy tasting. We hike over hill for 15 minutes to little lake for brook trout. Best tasting trout you'll ever get."

Well, they came close. But I still think the ultimate in brook trout eating has to do with tiny, spring-fed creeks boasting ice-cold water harboring lots of watercress. The trout from those places seem to taste nuttier and sweeter than brookies caught in some heavily-shaded waters. If taste and texture can vary so markedly in the same species, it just makes sense to catch your eating fish from waters producing the best flavors.

Q. I HAVE A PROBLEM WHEN I SAUTE MORE THAN ONE BATCH OF FISH. BY THE TIME THE SECOND PAN FULL OF FILLETS IS FINISHED COOKING THE FIRST BATCH HAS COOLED. HOW CAN I KEEP MY FISH HOT UNTIL I SERVE THEM?

A. Have a large heated serving platter ready to accommodate the pieces of fish the moment they are cooked. Use a heatproof platter (or metal baking pan) and set your stove's oven at 150 degrees. Line the platter with three layers of paper toweling, when the first batch is cooked, spread the pieces out on the toweling and put the platter in your oven. When the second batch is about cooked take the platter out. Stack the first pieces on one half of the platter. Put the second batch on the section of toweling that is now clear. Return the platter to the oven until you're ready to serve. If you have a lot of guests, use more than one platter and repeat the process.

Q. JUST ABOUT EVERYTHING I'VE READ ABOUT COOKING FISH CLAIMS THAT YOU SHOULD FRY FILLETS OVER HIGH HEAT FOR 10 MINUTES PER INCH OF THICK-NESS, TURNING ONLY ONCE. WHEN I DO THIS ... FIVE MINUTES PER SIDE ... THE SECOND SIDE IS ALWAYS OVER-

DONE. WHY IS THIS?

A. Because an uncooked piece of fish is cold when you first put it into a pan with hot oil. But it turns hot throughout while its first side is cooking. This means that when you flip the meat over the second side will cook much faster than the first side. This is where many chefs err and overcook their fish. You will do much better if you cook the first side six minutes, and the second side four minutes.

Q. DO YOU REALLY HAVE TO BE THAT PRECISE? ISN'T THERE AN EASIER WAY TO TELL WHEN FISH IS COOKED PERFECTLY?

A. Yes. Expert chefs watch their fish while it's cooking. They can tell when it's done by sight and touch. When sauteed and grilled fish turns golden crisp on both sides it's usually done. The touch test can prove it. Just press the fish. If the flesh is warm and soft, it's underdone. If it's hard and hot, it's overdone. If it's springy and firm, it's perfectly done. Through the years I've gained enough cooking experience to do the touch test with a spatula. I just press down on a cooking piece of fish with the spatula and make my decision. If there is any question as to degree of doneness I simply insert a corner of the spatula into the thickest part of the fish. A slight twist of my wrist tells me all I need to know. The flesh of perfectly cooked fish has become flaky, and it color has turned from translucent (raw) to opaque (cooked).

Q. IS THERE ANY KIND OF RULE FOR RECOMMENDED PORTIONS OF FISH? I ALWAYS SEEM TO COOK TOO MUCH OR TOO LITTLE.

A. Recommended serving sizes are based on species and method of cooking. In general, people tend to eat less of fish sauteed or fried than the same species when it's broiled. A 4 to 5-ounce serving of fried fish will satisfy most appetites, but it might take a strong 8 ounces of the same species if the meat is broiled. That's because broiled or grilled fish isn't nearly as filling.

Another consideration involves boneless vs bone-in fish. It will take 8 to 10 ounces of bone-in panfish to satisfy a hearty appetite, where 6 ounces will do the job if the meal consists of boneless fillets.

Still other considerations concern oily vs lean fish, and delicate vs firm-fleshed species. For example, you can eat a lot more lake perch than you can lake trout because the perch is lean and firm while lake trout flesh is oily and less firm. I'll have a lot more to say about these subjects in chapter 6.

Q. WHEN I FRY FISH FOR ONLY TWO OR THREE PEOPLE I SOMETIMES TRY TO GET THE JOB FINISHED WITH ONE COOKING SESSION. WHEN I'M WORKING WITH SMALL FILLETS IT'S EASY TO GET A LOT OF THEM INTO ONE BIG PAN. BUT WHEN I DO THIS I OFTEN FIND THE COOKED MEAT IS TOO GREASY. WHY DOES THIS HAPPEN?

A. The most important secret to getting perfectly crisp, grease-free fish is to fry just a few at a time. The more you crowd the pan the more you reduce the cooking temperature of the oil. The more you reduce that temperature as you add fillets the more oil they will absorb. Frying fish fast at high temperature keeps the juices in and the grease out. You will always have better eating if you fry in two batches instead of one because you'll be working with a high and even temperature of the oil.

Q. HOW CAN I TELL WHEN MY COOKING OIL IS HOT ENOUGH TO START FRYING?

A. Follow one of three general rules. You can heat your oil on high until it just barely begins to smoke, then add fish immediately. Some experts cooks prefer to heat oil hot enough to "spit back" when a drop of water is added. A better trick is to drop in a pinch of bread. If it fries instantly your oil is hot enough.

Q. I SEEM TO PREPARE GREAT FISH DINNERS WHEN I FRY PANFISH OR FILLETS FROM SMALLER PIKE AND WALLEYES. BUT WHEN I FRY THICKER PIECES FROM BIG-GER FISH MY RESULTS AREN'T NEARLY AS SATISFAC-TORY. WHY IS THIS?

A. Because when you are frying, the down side of the fillet is subject to intense heat. This means that it cooks very rapidly, which is why you have to flip the pieces over to cook both sides. But when you do this with a thick piece of meat you overcook the outside and undercook the interior because the inside doesn't reach a high enough temperature for the fillet to cook evenly.

It's best to remedy this problem by using a cooking method that subjects the entire piece of fish to a constant cooking temperature. It's a good rule of thumb to saute fish sections measuring up to 5/8-inch thick; and broil, bake, grill, poach or deep fry thicker sections. All of the latter methods utilize preheating of the cooking unit, which enables the meat to cook evenly.

Q. WHAT IS THE DIFFERENCE BETWEEN SAUTEING AND FRYING?

A. Cooks who use very little oil or grease are sauteing. Chefs who use a lot, say a cup or more of Crisco are frying, more than likely deep-frying. Many cooks, myself included, saute for health and taste reasons. The theory is the less grease coming in contact with food being cooked the less grease will be eaten. Also, because the flavor of fish is very delicate, the more grease you add to the fillet the more you can destroy that delicate flavor.

The argument could go on forever. It makes about as much sense as arguing the relative merits of well-done prime rib versus rare. Everybody has their personal tastes. You should cook your fish the way you like it.

Q. DO TYPES OF INGREDIENTS AND COOKING EQUIPMENT MAKE MUCH DIFFERENCE IN THE QUALITY OF MY FISH DINNERS?

A. Absolutely. For example, you can fry fish in margarine, but you shouldn't because it breaks down and burns too readily. One of the best chefs I know insists on peanut oil because it is relatively odorless and tasteless. That's excellent thinking , but there are other types of oil and grease designed for high-heat frying. I've tried lots of them, but I usually come back to plain Crisco or olive oil.

You can fry fish in just about any old frying pan, but you shouldn't. Heavy-gauge cast iron pans or heavy-duty electric frying pans hold even cooking temperatures in the high-heat range. This is mandatory because it's the only way to prevent cooking oils from absorbing into fish flesh.

And you can use pancake mix or variety of other heavy-content flours to coat your fillets, but again you shouldn't. Use flours designed specifically for frying fish, other seafood or chicken. The best I've found is Drake's, if you can get it. Most supermarkets in the Midwest and eastern states carry it, most western states don't. There are many other brands of thin-coat flour designed for high-temperature frying.

Q. WHENEVER I FRY FISH AT HIGH TEMPERATURE I GET A BAD "SPATTER" PROBLEM. HOW CAN I FRY MY FISH WITHOUT MAKING SUCH A MESS?

A. Spatter is produced by moisture coming into contact with hot grease. Reduce the moisture in your fillets and you'll reduce spatter. This is a particularly annoying problem with frozen fillets when it's necessary to defrost them in cold, running water. I put my thawed fish on several layers of newspaper to absorb much of the water. Then, just before cooking, I pat them dryer with paper toweling.

But considerable spatter is still a problem with all high-temperature frying. I usually saute my fish in the garage when I'm home. I spread out some newspaper on my work bench. I don't worry much about spatter because it lands on the newspaper which is later folded and tossed in the garbage can after cooking.

If you have to fry fish in the kitchen it can become a real problem. Nothing is more annoying then having to clean speckled grease spots off stove and counter tops.

The best answer is a lid large enough to completely cover your frying pan. The next best is to buy a spatter guard at your local supermarket.

Q. I'M A TROPHY BASS FISHERMAN BUT I LIKE TO EAT FISH TOO. I RELEASE MOST OF MY BIG BASS SO SOMEBODY ELSE CAN GET A THRILL CATCHING THEM, BUT OFTEN I'LL KEEP ONE FOR BROILING. THE ONLY SMALL BASS I KEEP ARE FISH THAT ARE HOOKED DEEP AND PROBABLY WON'T LIVE IF RELEASED. SO I OFTEN HAVE TO COOK FILLETS FROM BIG BASS AND LITTLE BASS AT THE SAME TIME. HOW COME THE SMALLER FISH ALWAYS TASTE BETTER?

A. Because table fare fades fast as age increases in all fish and game. The older the deer the tougher the chops. The older the bass the tougher and less flavorful the fillets. Liken the situation to what happens with sheep. Lamb chops are so good because they're taken from animals less than one year old when butchered. The smaller bass fillets taste so great because they come from young and therefore tender fish. You will always have better fish dinners if you keep the smaller fish and let the big ones go free, especially big northern pike which are always females. They can live to 25 years old, and they grow bigger and spawn more eggs every year.

Imagine the power of a 15 to 20-pound pike spurting away with speeds to 25 mph. Somebody coming behind you can get his or her thrill of a lifetime trying to harness that arm-jerking power with a spinning rod. There aren't many really big pike left, so let 'em go.

Q. HOW COME FISH DINNERS IN RESTAURANTS CAN VARY SO MUCH IN TASTE QUALITY. A BROILED WALLEYE SERVED IN ONE RESTAURANT CAN BE GREAT, BUT THE SAME DINNER SERVED IN ANOTHER EATERY MIGHT BE LOUSY. HOW CAN THIS BE?

A. Because quality control can vary tremendously in how fish is cared for and cooked. The worst story I ever heard in this regard came from a friend who worked in a restaurant kitchen. He once told me that when the cooks run out of expensive grouper, they'll often substitute inexpensive cod.

"It's easy to do, " Dan said. "We swaddle that cod in a tasty sauce that hides the switch. Most customers never guess."

When I told this story to Ted Jeveli, owner of a restaurant in East Boston, he practically bristled. "If you rip off a customer and he knows it he'll never come back." Ted said. "Usually, if a person remembers what he paid for a meal it wasn't good. If it's superb fish, and he gets all he can eat, he doesn't care what he paid because it was worth it. We don't disguise our fish in anything. We take the best care of it and cook it to perfection. True fish lovers determine over time which restaurants are tops. We have many customers who have been coming to Jeveli's for over 20 years."

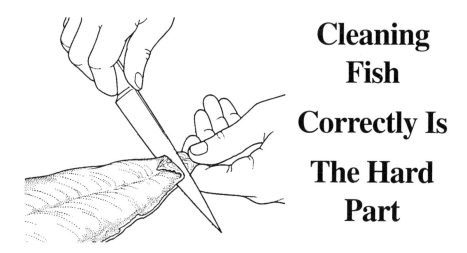

Cleaning Fish Correctly Is The Hard Part

Most fish will taste better if they are kept alive until you are ready to dress them. This is true because fish blood is a major contributor to strong fish flavor. Especially in sharks, the blood is so bad that unbled shark meat smells of ammonia. The blood of most saltwater fish, including the fast-swimming pelagics like tunas, mackerels and jacks, smells bad. The meat of these species can be vastly improved by bleeding. The best technique is to hang the fish overboard and kill it by cutting through the gill arches, which serve as a fish's lungs. The fish quickly pumps out most of its blood and dies within seconds.

Such bleeding of smaller species, including all panfish and most freshwater species, is impractical; that's why it's so important to keep them alive until cleaning. A fish that's killed with a sharp blow to the head, then cleaned immediately, bleeds itself during the cleaning process. If the fish-- or fillet-- is washed immediately, it becomes as blood free as it can get.

Another way to reduce the blood content of a fish's flesh, without going to much trouble, is to immediately place each catch in a fish box or cooler holding a generous supply of ice. The more ice, the greater the chilling effect. This is of prime importance because fast chilling draws the fish's blood to its internal organs, away from the fillets. Most anglers don't use enough ice to get the blood into internal organs fast and efficiently.

The colder the box the faster the blood drains. Even many charter boat captains skimp on ice. A single small bag won't do the job properly on big fish like salmon and lake trout. Put several 8-pound bags of party ice in your cooler. Such bags usually sell for less than one dollar each, a very cheap price to pay to make sure your fish are properly chilled.

If a fish isn't kept alive, or promptly chilled prior to cleaning, the blood stays in the flesh as the fish slowly dies. This is what happens to any catch that's put into a bucket of water, a fish box without ice, or strung on a stringer. The blood congeals in the flesh, and there is no way to remove it. Any fish cooked this way can't possibly reach its great flavorful potential because fish blood tastes bad.

Blood in the flesh is bad enough, but decomposition is even worse. It begins immediately after the fish dies. The warmer the weather, the faster the decomposing accelerates if the fish isn't iced. The breakdown of flesh and critical fish oils happens fast. Fishy flavors develop rapidly, making such poorly cared for fish bad table fare.

The only anglers who don't have to be concerned with such problems are ice fishermen. A winter fish caught through the ice begins chilling immediately after being unhooked and tossed on the ice. Many unknowing ice anglers probably wonder why there's little or no blood when they're filleting their catch. It's because the chilling effect of the ice has already drawn most of the blood into the internal organs. Again, without knowing why, many anglers prefer ice fishing over summer fishing because their fish taste better in winter.

Now we get to the hard pat ... cleaning your fish correctly. And it truly is the hard part of producing great fish dinners. My childhood learning process began with simply scaling bluegills, gutting them, cutting off heads, then frying them with bones and fins intact. I had to do it this way because I had no idea how to fillet a fish.

My education began when I met Bill Hoxie. He was in his mid-70s then, and had been a fanatic duck hunter. He just loved eating wild duck, but he couldn't hunt them anymore. When I discovered this I happily gave him a couple of cleaned mallards ready for roasting. It so happened that when I delivered the ducks to Bill's home he had just finished filleting a mess of crappies. He insisted I take a bunch of fillets in trade for the ducks.

Way back then my son was about eight years old. We didn't have many fish dinners because Jack wouldn't eat a piece of fish with bones. My wife would eat around a few of the bones because she loves fish. It was a whole different ball game when I fried the boneless fillets that Bill gave me. Jack took one to be polite, then got the surprise of his life when he began nibbling at it.

"Hey, Dad," he exclaimed, "there's no bones in this fish. It's really good!"

"Why don't you clean fish like this?" my wife added. "I'd much rather eat these crappie fillets than those ducks you bring home. Why don't you give Bill some more mallards? Trade 'em for fish."

I made my decision right there that I had to learn the art of filleting. The next day I visited Bill and asked if he would help me get started.

"Lets go catch us a bunch of crappies," he said with a welcome grin. "Then I'll show you how it's done."

He began my education while we were fishing. "Learning how to fillet fish really deserves a lot of effort," he said. "Any chore that doesn't have skill and time involved doesn't mean very much. You go down to the store and buy a steak and you don't even think about that steak recently being part of a living beef. But some skilled butcher had to think a lot about a lot of skills to get the steak out of a dead steer. Like a good butcher, a good filleter can amaze people with his skill in reducing a messy fish to clean meat. If you have to invest some of yourself into learning how to do it, it'll be worth a lot to you because your fish dinners will be so much better."

That's something I've believed in for a long time, over 40 years. That belief was reinforced just the other day when I drove down to the local dock where several Lake Michigan charter boats come in after a morning of salmon fishing. I noticed half a dozen men standing at the fish cleaning station, so I knew a boat captain was cleaning fish for his clients.

I walked up and watched the captain working with his knife. He was good, very good. His knife practically flew through those big salmon, making precise cuts with almost no effort. He was making slabs of fillets as fast as a couple of his clients could rinse and bag them.

When I see an act like that I know I'm watching a real pro because I know how much practice it takes to get that good. This guy had no doubt filleted thousands of fish during a long career, so I understood the humor in a remark he made.

One of his clients had piped up and said, "Boy, you sure clean fish in a hurry. Looks like you've done it before."

"No," the captain deadpanned, "actually this is only the second time I've tried it."

I think those guys believed him. Maybe they had never been fishing before. For sure they had no idea what a difficult art they were watching. I often take people fishing who say similar things to me when I'm filleting the day's catch. One of the most frequent remarks goes something like, "John, it's amazing how you make that knife work. You should have been a surgeon."

I utilize three fillet knives. Each matches the filleting job I'm undertaking. One has a short four-inch blade that's perfect for filleting perch and other small panfish. The next one has a six-inch blade that's ideal for pike, walleyes, smallmouth bass and saltwater species like snappers. The next knife up has an eight-inch blade. The blade on this knife is long enough to slice all the way through the depths of larger fish. I also use one knife designed only for skinning. A proper skinning knife comes with an offset blade designed to lay flat to the workbench surface, and it's much duller than razor-sharp filleting knives. The duller blade is far less likely to cut through skin. It's purpose is to shave skin, not cut it.

I thoroughly believe in going with top quality in filleting knives and sharpening equipment because they make the job so much easier. You can fillet a fish with a duller knife but its a tough process. If your knife is razor sharp it just glides through the meat with no dragging. Once you work with quality knives you'll slice many hours off a year's worth of filleting fish.

For much of my filleting career sharpening knives was a struggle. I finally developed system of using whetstones, but I never became proficient at the job. I purchased several different sharpening gadgets, but didn't hit paydirt until I acquired a diamond hone electric sharpener manufactured by Edgecraft Corporation. This sharpener hones and polishes the entire length of a cutting edge in three steps.

Each station on the sharpener has strong magnets that hold the knife blade at the precise angle for precision sharpening. Since I got my unit I've been amazed at how simple knife sharpening has become. The economy model costs about $48.

I can't emphasize too much how important a truly sharp knife is. A couple of days ago I caught three smallmouth bass. When I got home I found three business calls on my recorder. They needed quick response. I didn't want to monkey with putting those bass on ice, so I decided to clean them fast before returning the phone calls.

I took the fish to my outside cleaning table, killed them with my little club, then grabbed my filleting knife with the six-inch blade. With the first cut I knew I should have sharpened the knife. But the sharpener was back in the garage. I was in a hurry and the knife blade was already in the fish, so I just kept cutting. The first fillet came off with ragged edges and too much meat left on the backbone. "Man, I said to myself, "I'm glad nobody's around to see how I screwed up this job.

For maybe the 100th time in recent years I realized that I was trying to clean a fish with a knife that wasn't sharp enough to do a good job. It made no sense trying to clean those bass correctly until I took the time to sharpen the knife and relax. I put them in a bucket, filled it half full with cold well water, dumped in some ice cubes, and went into my office to make phone calls.

When I got back in the garage I sharpened that knife to point where I could probably shave with it. When I sliced the second fillet off that bass the blade just glided along smoothly through flesh and rib bones with no hang-up at all. That's the way it's suppose to feel.

The next most important item is your cleaning station. Your filleting table should be standard workbench height. Trying to work off low tables -- such as picnic tables -- will guarantee a sore back in short order. My table is topped with a 4-foot by 3-foot piece of hard plastic that is half-inch thick. I got it from a butcher friend who uses it on all his meat-cutting benches. Any cutting board will do the job if you don't fillet a lot of fish. Hard plywood makes a good work surface, and you can cut it any size you want. It's easy to clean, and contributes to holding fish steady while you're working on them. Another great surface is the counter top material used in kitchens.

You'll add greatly to the flavor of your fish if you keep your cleaning table sanitary. I keep a hose handy, and I wash off my table several times while filleting a single batch of fish. This reduces the amount of bacteria-infested scales, stomach juices or droppings that could come into contact with my fillets. Rinsing off the table with water every few minutes is a great habit to form.

I also utilize a bucket of clean water and a big bowl about half full of ice cubes. Each fillet I remove from a carcass gets rinsed in the water to remove any remaining blood, then I put it into the bowl of ice cubes. The rinsing-- whether the fillet is skinned or not-- helps remove unwanted juices in addition to blood. The icing helps to firm the meat and keep it chilled.

Most fish have fatty tissues in the bottom of the belly, along the lateral line, and above the tops of the backbone. These fat tissues are darker colored than the rest of the flesh. Most contaminants are also in the fatty portions. No fish dinner can possibly be great unless these tissues are cut away because they impart a strong fishy flavor when cooked.

Some guides and experienced anglers handle the belly fat problem with a single slice of the knife. They simply cut the bottom of the belly off before beginning the next filleting operations. Other filleters, the really good ones, can eliminate the rib bones with their next cut which is the normal first cut.

Begin behind the gills and just behind the front fin sockets. Slice straight down to the backbone. Then, without removing the blade, turn it 90 degrees so it's laying on the backbone. Now slice straight along the backbone toward the tail. The experts, when they make this cut, slice right over the rib bones, leaving them still attached to the backbone. You have to know exactly where those bones are in the skeleton of the fish to be able the make this cut. You also have to "feel" the sharp edge of the blade actually riding over the ribs. It's a complicated cut but it eliminates any chance of cutting intestines. The people who can make it probably filleted many hundreds of fish before they developed the knack.

Most of us just make the complete cut -- which is standard procedure with panfish and other smaller fish -- you have now cut the first fillet free from the carcass. Now flip the fish over and repeat the procedure.

This is the fastest way to get fillets off a fish, but you still have to remove the rib sections. This operation requires a sharp, flexible blade, which is one reason why good fillet knives are made with their unique design. Slide the blade under the top of the rib bones and slice away the entire bony section. Some folks don't want to waste the extra meat that's thrown away with the bones, so they make an extra cut. Start at the top of the rib bones, slice down and away along the outside edges of the bones until you have sliced them away from the flesh. This cut gives you a little more meat and trimmer looking fillet.

There's one last cut needed to remove the skin. Insert the flat knife blade at the tail (narrow) end of your fillet. Press it against the cleaning table and cautiously "saw" the blade back and forth until you have made a parallel cut between meat and skin that measures about an inch. Press a finger or thumb against the flap of skin so you can hold the fillet in place, then rapidly "shave" the meat away from the skin.

With bigger fish it's standard technique to skin the fillet before cutting it free from the carcass. Make the first cut along the backbone to within about an inch of the tail. Flip the fillet over length wise so it's straight out from the test of the fish. Hook your left index finger (if you're right handed) under the hinge of skin still holding the fillet to the tail section. This is done so you can anchor the whole fillet from sliding on the work surface while you're making the "sawing" cut that runs between the skin and flesh. Once this cut is made it's time to remove the rib cages in the manner already discussed.

The next level of expertise in filleting involves removing the small bones you didn't get with the basic cutting strokes. Most fish have a row of bones running lengthwise down the center of the fillet. They're referred to as "pin bones" by anyone who knows the skeleton structure of fish. They're small, short bones in panfish and other smaller fish. Many anglers who know only a few basics of filleting don't even try to get them out of the fillet because they don't know how.

You can feel the tips (sharp points) of these bones barely sticking out of the fillet for about half its length. Remove them by cutting a "zip strip." It's done by making a V-shaped narrow cut on both sides of the bones, then pulling out the bone-filled V with your fingers. You can use this meat-bone combination for making stock. The cut in itself only goes half the length of the fillet, so no harm is done to the rest of the meat.

There's a better way of getting rid of these bones, but you have to have knowledge of the skeleton structure of the fish to make the cut. Begin by making the initial slice behind the fin's next to the gills. This cut goes vertically down to the backbone. This makes it easier for you to make the next cut that goes down along the dorsal fin and backbone, beginning at the head end of the fish where you made the first vertical cut. The cut continues along the backbone (but just above the rib bones) until the knife tip passes a point opposite the anus.

Now push the blade (still in a horizontal position) straight through the fish until the tip is out the other side. At this point work the blade in a sawing motion along the backbone until you have cut the fillet loose from the skeleton at the tail. Now the only thing holding the fillet to the rest of the fish is the meat around the pin bones and the rib bones. When you know where those pin bones are you can slide the tip of the blade right under them. An upward twist of the blade's sharp edge will then pop them loose from the meat. Now cut down to the rib bones and carve along their outside edges until you free the entire fillet from the skeleton. This cut also eliminates cutting into the intestines, which is a major no - no!

Is all this beginning to sound a little too complicated? I can make it sound even worse by telling you that pin bones in northern pike, chain pickerel and muskies have three ends instead of two. Cutting these demons out takes even more knowledge. See box for how it's done:

My written instruction about how to cut up fish is far from the best way to learn. You'll discover tricks of the trade fastest by watching an expert demonstrate how the cuts are made. Some of the larger membership fishing clubs hire pros to come to their clubs. They cut up fish the members catch and donate for the lessons. A real pro can throw a big bass on a table, whip out a knife, and within 30 seconds be finished filleting the fish.

How do these guys get that good? Well, consider that two or three butchers in a busy fish market will fillet more than 1,000 pounds of fish in a single day. As with everything else, practice makes perfect.

Many restaurants buy their fish whole. This means the chefs have to fillet them before they're cooked. If you know one of these guys, and can get him to help you, you can become an expert filleter in a hurry. Another

CUTTING OUT Y-BONES

Removing Y-bones from northern pike fillets is easy after a bit of practice. Cut off and skin both fillets. Place one fillet on cleaning table, skinned side down. Remove rib bones as discussed earlier. Then cut lengthwise through the fillet with knife blade exactly following the lateral line. The lower piece of meat is now bone free. Set aside.

The upper piece contains the Y-bones. Feel for them by running your finger --lengthwise-- along the thickest part of the remaining meat. The bone tips you feel are the outside prongs of the Y-bone. Place your knife blade parallel to and tight against these bone tips. Slice down and angling out along the edges of these bones, continually guiding the blade lengthwise along bones through entire strip of meat.

You now have two strips of meat. The dorsal side is bone free. The strip from the middle of the fillet (see outlined section in sketch) contains the Y-bones. I slice these strips into 3 to 4-inch sections and freeze them for later pickling. The pickling process disintegrates the bones. Pickled pike is a gourmet treat.

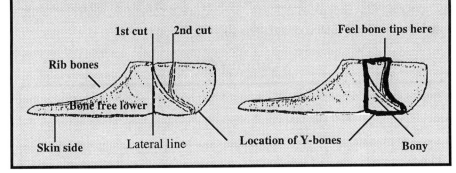

good bet is to pay full attention when guides or charter-boat captains fillet the day's catch.

Practically all good filleters learn their skills from somebody who already knows them. Years ago I thought I was pretty skillful when I met a new outdoorsman who just moved to town. This guy came from Chicago. I didn't think any big-city dude could show me anything new about hunting or fishing. Boy, was I wrong. Ted taught me a lot, including how to fillet the Y-bones out of northern pike. If you can make friends with a guy like Ted, you'll become a good filleter in short order. You'll also become a better angler, making it possible to choose the few fish you want to eat and releasing the rest.

After you have studiously watched several good filleters at work you'll notice that there is no one-best technique. Each expert can do the job with different strokes and still wind up with identical fillets.

I watched this happening one day last winter at the charter-boat section of a marina in Florida. I showed up shortly after the boats arrived at their 5:00 pm quitting time. The first chore for all the captains was cleaning the day's catch for their clients.

There were four cleaning tables in a row. Each was occupied by a captain filleting at least two different species of fish. I noted that each was using a different series of cutting strokes than the one I prefer. Then I noticed another captain, still in his boat, filleting fish on a portable cutting board. I watched in fascination because he was using the same cutting strokes that I was taught over 40 years ago.

All of these guys took about the same amount of time to fillet a fish, wash the meat, cut it into 3-inch pieces and store it in plastic bags ready for coolers. This is typical filleting procedure, except for small fish which usually are sliced into 2 equal size fillets.

Skinning fillets

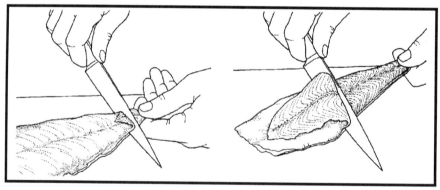

Make a small cut at the narrow end of the fillet and grab the skin. Use a sharp knife, held parallel to the skin, to run between the skin and flesh.

Different ways to cut up fish

DRAWN: The fish is whole except for being gutted and scaled. Large whole fish are usually baked, grilled, steamed or poached.

DRESSED: The fish is still in one piece but its head, tail, fins, scales and viscera have been removed. Small dressed fish are usually sauteed or deep fried.

STEAKS: These cuts are cross-section slices about 1 to 1½-inches thick. The backbone and skin have not been removed. Steaks can be cooked by any method, but need added moisture (usually marinades) when grilled or broiled. Before steaking remove scales, guts, bloodline and dorsal fin.

Trim away fatty tip ends of steak.

FILLETS: The fish has been cut lengthwise, along the backbone. When done carefully and with skill, the results are skinless and boneless pieces of 100 percent pure meat. These superb cuts can be cooked by any method but usually need moist heat because they tend to dry out quickly. One of the best possible fish dinners comes from properly sauteed fillets.

FINGERS: Any fillet can be cut crosswise into fingers of almost any size, but they are usually cut 1/2 to 1-inch wide. They make easy and quick sauteing or deep frying.

Thoughts On Cooking Methods

The problem in being a professional fish chef is the expectations of guests invited for dinner. They often expect fancy, multi-course meals. Nothing could be further from the way I entertain. My overall theme is to keep it simple and use the freshest ingredients. This translates into fresh-caught fish, fresh-picked or fresh-purchased vegetables and a simple cooking method. The hands-on work in my fish dinners seldom exceed 30 minutes, and that includes meals often planned at the last minute.

At the other extreme, cooking fish can be as complicated as you care to make it. There are as many different recipes for each species as there are species in the waters. What I've described in this chapter are the easiest—but tastiest—procedures for the most succulent fish dinners I know how to cook.

I saute about 50 percent of my fish because sauteing is the best method of cooking panfish fillets, all other small fillets no more than 5/8-inch thick, and fish "fingers" cut crosswise from fillets of any size. Sauteed fish should be lightly coated (dusted) with a seasoned flour and cooked in about two tablespoons of Crisco or canola or olive oil at about 375 degrees. This is by far the best way to bring out the delicate flavors of small pieces of fish.

By varying the coating, the oil or grease, the species of fish, and accompanying side dishes, you could saute fish twice a week for months without repeating yourself.

It's impossible to properly saute unless you use relatively dry pieces of fish because excessive moisture will produce steam. Not only do you steam instead of fry your fish, but you also cause excessive spatter. Both situations prevent pieces of fish from coming out crisp and tender. The problems are partially licked by draining your fillets on paper toweling or newspaper for 10 minutes or so before cooking. Such draining is effective on all fillets, even those that are soaking wet from defrosting in cold, running water.

The trick in cooking fish by any method is to cook it thoroughly without overdoing. Minutes count big time when preparing fish because it cooks so quickly. If fish becomes overcooked it will be mealy, tough and dry. Properly sauteed fish should come out moist, crisp, and tender but NOT BURNED. Those are the two key words. Cook the first sides of each fillet until they are golden crisp, usually about three to four minutes, then flip them. Your fillets are overcooked if they have turned a deep, rich brown.

I honestly believe it took me many years to learn that most basic lesson. If I was teaching a newcomer how to saute fish today I would deliberately overcook a few fillets to dramatically prove the taste difference between GOLDEN CRISP and deep, rich brown. To become comfortable with sauteing you have to keep "doing it", cooking and tasting each piece until you begin savoring every delicious mouthful.

Deep frying is an extremely popular method of cooking fish. If you like heavy batters, deep frying is the way to go because it's done in a large quantity of hot oil designed to cook the entire surface of each piece of fish. The heavy batter cooks almost instantly and locks in the flavor and moisture that assures crispness. But remember to cook HOT, at least 350 degrees. You will just have a greasy mess if you try to deep fry at lower temperatures. But don't go too hot. Most fats and oils will burn at over 400 degrees. Done correctly, deep-frying creates a delectable crisp coating that can't be duplicated by other cooking methods.

There are two major ways to insure success. Use enough oil, at least 1-1/4 inches to completely submerge each piece of fish. But less is best when it comes to other deep frying ingredients. Throw away all the batter recipes that call for a dozen different ingredients. Experiment with several of the thicker-mix batters made especially for frying fish or chicken. You'll find several in any major supermarket. Select one that best suits your taste.

Now you are ready to fry fish to perfection every time, as long as you don't pay too much attention to a popular fish-frying myth. That rule of thumb says a piece of fish cooking in a deep fryer is done when it floats in the oil.

"That's bad advice," says Ted Jeveli, my good friend who owns Jeveli's restaurant in East Boston. Ted's place seats 240 diners, serves 4,200 meals per week and has 70 employees. Many of those people are chefs who cook fish, a lot of fish. "It's certainly true that deep-fried fish is done when it floats," Ted went on. "It's also overdone to the point where it's getting tougher every second it keeps floating."

"The secret to perfect deep-fried fish is to get the pieces out of the oil as soon as they begin showing signs of buoyancy. We tell our chefs not to wait until the fish pieces are floating because by then it's too late for top quality."

Here are more frying suggestions. Fry only those fish that are most suitable for frying. Most freshwater species fit this category because they are lean. Medium to heavy oil-content fish (salmon, lake trout, steelhead and whitefish) are best cooked with other methods. Small stream trout are low in oil content, therefore they're great for sauteing. Other top choices include walleye, pike, and all panfish. About the best fish dinner possible is a mess of fresh-caught lake perch sauteed to perfection.

Don't add too many pieces of fish to the hot oil at the same time. If you cool the oil too rapidly with too many pieces, the fish will soak up the grease and taste greasy. It's imperative to fry hot whether sauteing or deep frying, so add fillets or pieces in steady succession, but only one piece at a time. You should also preheat your pan 4 or 5 minutes. Only just before frying should you add the fat.

54

Yes, you can saute in the electric frypan because it's a great device that offers that capability. But you can deepfry, too. So if you own a top quality electric frypan you have all the equipment you need for all the fish frying you'll ever want to do. You can't get much simpler than that. Once again I'll point out that frying fish correctly can be a pretty simple process, as long as you always remember to fry HOT. If a pinch of bread fries instantly when dropped into hot oil, you oil is hot enough.

The biggest mistake in serving fried fish is letting it cool before it gets to the table. As fried fish cools, it absorbs moisture from the air and crispness diminishes. Keep cooked fish warm in your oven until dinner is served.

I mentioned a few paragraphs back that salmon, lake trout and steelhead are not the best species for sauteing or deep-frying because they're too oily. But here's a handy tip for making these fish less oily if you prefer to fry them.

After your fish have been filleted, measure 3 tablespoons of table salt and 2 teaspoons of baking soda into 1 gallon of cold water. Stir until dissolved. Submerge the fish in this solution and refrigerate overnight.

The next morning you'll find the brine covered with a floating layer of oil and slime. Discard the used saltwater, rinse the fillets in cold water and dry on paper toweling before frying. The guy that told me about this system feels that fried fish is so superior to fish cooked with other methods that he goes to great lengths to prepare them perfectly.

Another handy tip involves the sauteing of unskinned panfish fillets, particularly perch. Always cook the first side skin up because "skin up" holds in moisture and flavor and helps prevent curling.

Here are some ideas on the gourmet side of fish frying. Some chefs claim it's not how well you fry fish, but how you serve it once it's fried. One of my friends lays out his deep-fried fillets on a Pyrex dish, smothers them in sauteed onions, then places the works in a pre-heated 450 degree oven for 3 minutes. That's all it takes for the flavor of the onions to blend into the seasoned batter.

Here's a recipe I got in Mexico while on a Dove hunt. It has a Tex-Mex flavor.

> 1 pound small bass fillets
> 2 tablespoons margarine
> 1 medium tomato, chopped, about 1 cup
> 1 small green pepper chopped, about 1/2 cup
> 2 tablespoons finely chopped fresh cilantro or parsley
> 1/4 cup dry white wine

Saute fish 4 to 6 minutes, turning once. Remove fillets to warm platter. Cook remaining ingredients (except wine) over medium heat 3 to 5 minutes, stirring frequently, until pepper and onion are crisp tender. Stir in wine and heat until hot. Spoon mixture over fish. Serves four.

Fresh produce always goes great with fried fish. Try these excellent combinations.

> 1-1/2 pounds sauteed panfish
> 1-1/2 pounds baby red potatoes
> 1 pound green peas
> 2 tablespoons butter or margarine

Scrub potatoes but do not peel. Cut small ones in half, quarter larger ones. Place in pan with enough water to cover. Bring to a boil. Cover an simmer for 12 minutes. Add peas. Return to boil and simmer about 5 minutes, or until vegetables are tender. Add butter and desired seasonings. Serve hot fish and vegetables on warm plates.

Here's another favorite of mine utilizing panfish fillets.

> 2 pounds panfish fillets
> 1/2 cup green onions, chopped
> 1 garlic clove, minced
> 1/2 cup unpeeled cucumber, chopped
> 1/2 cup dry white wine

Saute onions and garlic in 2 tablespoons Crisco or oil until tender. Remove from pan and set aside. Saute fillets in remaining oil. Add seasonings of choice, wine, cucumber and cooked vegetables. Cover and simmer 3 to 4 minutes. Remove everything from pan with slotted spatula and serve on warm plates. Serves four.

I've encountered many expert anglers who are also excellent cooks because they have cooked so many fish over so many years. One theme that keeps coming up is the wonderful taste that milk or buttermilk adds to sauteed or fried fish. I personally don't believe that top quality fish can be improved by adding unnatural ingredients. So I don't use milk in any form, but here's one way it's done if you want to try it.

    4 6-ounce skinned and boneless fillets of most any good fish
    1/2 cup Drakes or any good frying flour
    1 tablespoon grated lemon peel, optional
    1 teaspoon Cayenne pepper, optional
    3 tablespoons Crisco or oil
    2/3 cup buttermilk

Combine flour, lemon peel, cayenne pepper and other desired seasonings in grocery bag. Shake until well mixed. Pour buttermilk into shallow dish. Dip fillets in buttermilk until soaked, add to flour and shake contents until each fillet is well coated. Saute or fry to desired doneness.

I'll mention another unnatural ingredient my sister swears by. She drives 250 miles (one way) to my home in northern Michigan just to catch crappies and cook the fillets with her special recipe. She calls the result "scrumptious". She cooks all her panfish the same way every time, and calls them "Walnut-crusted crappies".

    12 crappie fillets skinned and boned
    1/2 cup flour
    2 egg whites
    3/4 cup walnuts, minced
    4 tablespoons Crisco or oil
    1 lemon, quartered

Rinse the fillets, pat dry, and dredge in flour mixed with desired seasonings. Beat egg whites lightly. Dip floured fillets in egg whites, then into minced walnuts, coating each piece thoroughly. Set the fillets aside and heat Crisco or oil to medium-high temperature in 12-inch skillet.

Saute 6 fillets about 4 minutes on first side and 3 minutes on second side. Repeat with second batch. Garnish with lemon wedges. Serves four.

Here's a similar recipe that works better with larger fish producing fillets measuring about 5/8-inch thick at their thickest part.

> 4 6-ounce skinless boneless walleye or bass fillets
> 4 tablespoons oil
> 1/2 tablespoon lemon juice
> 2 tablespoons minced roasted hazelnuts
> seasoning of choice

Blend 1/2 oil, lemon juice and hazelnuts in small pan, set aside. Add 1/2 oil to 12-inch skillet and heat to almost smoking. Place 2 fillets in pan and saute 5 minutes on first side and 3 minutes on second side. Repeat with other 2 fillets while hazelnut mixture is heating to hot, then pour over fillets, Serves four. Tip: To quickly mince hazelnuts or walnuts, drop the nuts through a tube of a food processor with the motor running.

Tip No. 2 for these recipes: The nutty flavors go especially well with the first fresh asparagus of early spring. The thinner the spears, the better. Snap off the tough lower ends of the spears where they break easily. Rinse, place in wide skillet, just cover with water. Bring to a boil, reduce heat and simmer about 8 minutes or until tender-crisp.

The next best time to try these recipes is late summer when the first new tomatoes are ripening in the garden. Fresh sliced and marinated new tomatoes are always a good bet with any fish dinner. Slice the tomatoes and spread on a serving platter. Top with sliced onions, then marinate with any liquid salad dressing of your choice.

New potatoes, boiled, chunked, then topped with butter and small pieces of parsley make a delicious and colorful part of eating fish. So do thick slices of Italian or French bread spread with butter, topped with salt free Lawry's or McCormick garlic and herb seasoning, and heated in your microwave for 15 seconds to blend the flavors.

Herbed rice is another great and simple embellishment for fish. Just mix some chopped green onions (green tops included), chopped chives or minced basil in with the rice before cooking. Fluff the works with a fork before serving. Thinly sliced fresh cucumbers or summer squash go great with any fish dinner.

As I mentioned earlier I saute or fry about 50 percent of the fish I cook. My next preference is grilling, then comes broiling. That's why I devote the next two chapters to these techniques. I almost never cook fish by blackening, baking, planking, steaming or oven-frying. That leaves poaching and braising. Occasionally I use both methods.

Poaching is best done in a court bouillon (koor bwee-YAWN) that covers the pieces of fish. Braising is a method of cooking that is halfway between sauteing and poaching, but the fish is only partially covered with liquid. The flavored cooking liquid is the key ingredient with both methods because it imparts delicious tastes produced by simmering vegetables and herbs.

No matter which species of game fish you catch in your region you can poach or braise them with almost guaranteed success because the system is so forgiving. You can't overcook poached or braised fish, and it's healthy cooking because you use no fats or oils. Here is my recipe for a court bouillon.

    2 carrots cut in chunks
    1 large onion, chopped
    1 lemon wedge
    1 tablespoon chopped chives or parsley
    1 bay leaf
    8 cups water

Simmer vegetables and herbs together 45 minutes, then bring to a boil and add enough fish for 4 servings. The boiling sears the outside of the pieces, keeps them from falling apart and seals in the juices. As soon as the fish goes in it's important to reduce heat to a simmer. Cook 8 to 10 minutes. Too much boiling tends to make fish fall apart. Poaching always produces a silky-textured piece of fish. You can poach in any pot or pan big enough to hold all the ingredients. Most ideal is a roasting pan with a rack that enables lifting out the fish pieces after cooking, otherwise use a slotted spatula.

The main difference between poaching and braising is the control of flavor. Because braising uses less liquid you can literally soak in stronger and more delicious flavors. If you have a vegetable garden you have a gold mine of flavors available for braising. I'm going to borrow 3 paragraphs from my venison cookbook BEST VENISON EVER to prove how strongly I feel about this situation.

"My appreciation of the power of fresh vegetables always peaks when I make kabobs with just picked vegetables from my garden. It's difficult to explain why this combination produces such magic, but I'll give it a try.

"One time I took a venison shoulder roast from my freezer, thawed it then cut bite-size pieces of meat from the choicest section. I had more meat than I could use for the kabobs I was making, so I put the extra pieces in the refrigerator. Then I made the kababs, broiled the works and sat down to a meal that was so complete and satisfying that it could be termed nothing less than superlative.

"The next day my wife sauted those extra pieces of meat. They didn't measure up to the taste quality of the meat in the kabobs, even though both groups were cut from the same roast. Why? The only possible answer is that the clear, uncomplicated and delicate flavors of those super-fresh vegetables worked into the kabobs meat while cooking."

You can do the same thing, only better, while poaching or braising fish. While poaching is done in a large stockpot or roasting pan, you can braise in the bottom of a casserole or large skillet while using only an inch or so of liquid. This process is the absolute best way of infusing those delicate flavors of super-fresh vegetables into fish because all the flavors ar concentrated in small volumes of liquid.

The easiest way of doing this is to save the liquid resulting from steaming or boiling vegetables. You can use it fresh or freeze it for later use. Braising inspires a creative sense of seasoning, too. You can combine freshly chopped vegetables with a flavorful broth so that maximum flavor is gently cooked into lean fish. Braising, without question, is one of the easiest and most versatile ways to cook delicious fish.

Experiment with different mixtures of vegetables and seasonings. I like to saute thin slices of onions with chopped red or green peppers to make a thin base in the bottom of a skillet. I top that with 3-inch wide pieces of walleye or smallmouth bass fillets, then add the saved broth from cooking almost any fresh vegetables. The idea is to use enough liquid to cover about half the thickness of the fish, but not to submerge it. Bring the works to a boil , reduce heat to a simmer, cover to hold in the flavors, and cook gently for about 10 minutes.

Another favorite of mine is to layer the bottom of the skillet with finely chopped carrots, green onions and celery cooked to about half tender in 4 to 5 minutes. Add fish pieces and broth and simmer 10 more minutes.

The combinations are almost endless. All fresh veggies infuse magnificent flavors into lean fish. Braising is perhaps the greatest way to cook fish indoors on rainy summer days because there's no smell. The only drawback to poached or braised fish is that it can be a bit bland. A good tartar sauce with a little zing is the answer. Leftovers are always great because no fat or oil is used in the cooking. Remember, though, that natural fat cooks out of oily fish during all poaching or braising. Never reuse this liquid in other cooking.

Some Important Things To Know About Cooking Fish

The chart on the following page shows the best way to cook your catch. Fish with high fat contents are not suitable for frying. Saute, deep fry, grill and broil are the best cooking methods.

X - Indicates the common ways to cook.

√ - Indicates the best ways to cook.

	Low fat content (lean)	Moderate fat	High fat (oily)	Soft Texture	Moderate firm	Firm	Saute	Deep fry	Grill	Poach	Braise	Broil	Bake
LargemouthBass	X				X		√	√	√	X	X	X	X
Smallmouth Bass		X				X	√	√	√	X	X	X	X
Northern Pike		X					√	√				X	√
Walleye	X				X		√	√	X			X	X
Sunfish	X					X	√						
Bluegill	X					X	√					X	
Yellow Perch	X					X	√						
Stream Trout		X			X		√		√				
Steelhead			X		X				√	X	X	√	X
Coho Salmon			X	X					√	X	X	√	X
Chinook Salmon			X		X				√	X	√	√	X
Atlantic Salmon			X		X				√	X	X	√	
Lake Trout			X		X				√	X	X	√	
Whitefish		X		X						√		√	X
Crappie		X			X		√					X	
Catfish		X			X		X	√	X				
White Bass	X				X		√	X	X		X		
Snapper		X			X		√	√				X	X
Sea Trout		X		X			√	√			X	X	X
Tuna			X			X			√	X	X		
Mahi-Mahi	X					X			√	X	X	X	X
Grouper	X					X	√	√	√	X	X	X	X
Shark	X					X			√			X	
Swordfish			X			X			√			X	X
Cod	X			X			X	√		X	X	√	√
Wahoo	X					X			√			√	
Mackerel		X			X				√	X	X	√	
Sheepshead		X				X	√	√		X	X	X	
Flounder	X				X		X		X			√	X
Orange Roughy	X					X	√	√					
Ocean Perch		X						√	X			X	X
Halibut	X				X		X	X	X		X	√	
Pompano			X					√	X	X		√	√
Grunt	X						√	√		X	X		
Haddock	X			X			√	√				√	√
Bluefish (North)			X		X				√	X	X	√	
Marlin			X		X				√	X	X	X	X
Snook		X				X	X		√			√	
Redfish		X			X		X		√		X	√	

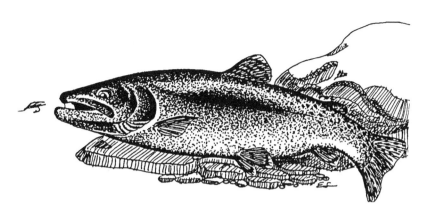

Grilling Great Dinners

Some years ago I was surf casting for brown trout along the shoreline of Lake Michigan. It was early spring when the shoreline shallows were warming enough to attract smelt, which in turn attract brown trout. I don't fish in one place. I wade slowly along shore, casting my spinners or spoons.

Eventually I noticed another fellow doing the same thing. I was going north while he was wading south, so we soon closed to within talking range.

"How're you doing?" I asked.

"Nothin' yet. But I'll get at least one, I get some trout every day."

"Every day? You fish here every day?"

"Not always here. But somewhere in this vicinity. I'm between jobs, so I fish. I've got a job waiting out in Lake Tahoe May 1st. But I'm running out of money, so I fish as much to eat as I do for fun."

This fellow was really interesting, so I quit fishing to talk.

"If you catch trout every day you get more than you can eat;" I went on. "What do you do with 'em?"

"I release most . I've got a first-floor 1-bedroom apartment. There's a gas grill outside. When people from other apartments aren't using it I grill my brown trout dinners. I can't afford to buy meat. Besides, I think grilled trout is better eating than most steak you can buy. And grilling fish is so simple. I don't mess with flour and grease and frying pans. And I get variety in dinners without much expense."

"Oh. How do you do that?"

"Fresh vegetables are about the cheapest food you can buy, and they work great for adding various flavors to fish. For example, tonight I'll put a trout fillet on a sheet of tinfoil, top it with a few slices of onions or silvers of garlic, wrap the works up and put it on the hot grill. In about 15 minutes I'm eating a fresh brown trout fillet grilled to perfection. Sometimes I'll spread a bit of mayonnaise or mustard on the fillet, then top that with thin slices of cucumber or tomato. Often I'll take the cooked fish out of the foil and put in chunked asparagus, potato, most any vegetable. They'll steam cook in a hurry, and I'll have a great meal!"

With all that said, I'll go to the other extreme and tell you that cooking fish on the grill tends to confuse many outdoor cooks. There's mystery involved that doesn't exist with the burgers, steaks and hot dogs that are grilled frequently. But fish on the grill? Most backyard cooks shy away from it. There are too many memories of fillets falling through the grill grates, collapsing off spatulas or winding up dry and tough. How can a food that's otherwise so quick and easy to prepare turn into such a disaster when exposed to hot coals?

Fear is the culprit. Fish is far from the easiest food to grill when you don't know how. Once you learn how it's done you'll find that grilling is one of the best and easiest ways to cook fish. As soon as you get armed with the proper knowledge your cooking and eating life will be immeasurably enriched.

Grilling fish is like cleaning fish. If you don't do it right you have a mess. In both operations the key word is RELAX. There's something about fire that makes people think it's an emergency. You can be a most successful fish griller if you use some patience and a bit of experimentation. The basic advice is to start simply and think meat.

For the beginner it's best to cook fish steaks. They're easiest to get on and off the grill and they cook in the same way you cook beefsteaks, only faster. Salmon are made to order for slicing into steaks. Cut them at least one-inch thick. Lake trout and steelhead make great steaks. So do some salt water fish. Thick sections of Mahi-Mahi can be cut into steaks resembling pork chops. Other "steak-fish" species include tuna, sword-fish and Mako shark. Fish steaks are great when you're learning because the bones and skin keep the meat from falling apart. The skin also partially protects the meat from burning and drying out. Finally, even if you make mistakes, the meat still won't stick to the grill any more than chicken breasts.

If you don't have any fish steaks, and you won't be going fishing for awhile, you can buy Atlantic salmon steaks in most any supermarket. Of all commercial fish you can purchase, your best bet for freshness is usually Atlantic salmon. (See chapter 12 for more details).

Your goal in grilling salmon steaks is to cook the meat so that it's crispy golden on the outsides and moist within. Begin by heating a marinade consisting of one-third lemon juice and two-thirds margarine. Make enough of this mixture to easily brush coat both sides of the number of steaks you will grill. Use a small brush (a one-inch cheap paint brush is ideal) to coat both sides of steaks. The old guide who gave me this recipe said to marinate your fish steaks about the same amount of time it takes

HOW TO TELL WHEN FISH IS COOKED

Every fish cookbook ever written says that fish is properly cooked when the meat has turned opaque and flakes easily when tested with the tip of a knife or fork. I've been asked many times just what is meant by opaque and flaking.

Opaque means that the color of the flesh has turned from a raw to cooked appearance. With properly cooked salmon the color has changed from orange to a light beige. When the orange is gone the steak is cooked, maybe overcooked because hot fish will continue cooking for several minutes after being removed from the grill. Retained heat causes this situation, so it's best to slightly under cook. If you under cook too much you can easily put the steaks back on the grill for a minute or so.

Flaking means simply that cooked fish will easily split along its natural separations when tested with a knife tip or fork.

to drink a beer, say about half an hour.

While doing this preheat your gas grill by turning both burners on high. Remove grate and wire brush it until clean. Spray it with no-stick cooking spray, then return it to grill. Turn burners down to about medium, close cover. When steaks are marinated, place them on sprayed grate which should be positioned about four to five inches above coals. Cook about five minutes, occasionally inserting a metal spatula between flesh and grill to prevent sticking. Turn steaks and cook another three to four minutes, again working spatula in and out and side to side to make sure fish doesn't stick. At this point, check for doneness.

Here are some more tips.

Keeping fish from sticking to the grate is the biggest problem in grilling seafood. The trick is to thoroughly clean the grate before cooking because cooked-on food particles cause fish to stick. The best procedure is to wire brush the grids clean, then either spray or brush them with cooking oil. Many experienced cooks wire brush the grate while it's in place on the grill. Others don't like to do this because they don't want the brushed off food particles inside their fire box. Just remember that the grate must be hot before you put steaks on it.

If you leave it in place for the cleaning job it's imperative that you brush on the cooking oil instead of spraying. Many spray-on oils are inflammable. Your can make a huge error by spraying this stuff into hot coals. I prefer to spray my grate away from the grill, then get it hot. Other experienced fish cooks claim it's best to clean the grate in place, heat it for several minutes, then brush it with oil. Either way works perfectly.

To be sure that thick steaks cook through, it's best to cook over medium heat. I also like to cover the grill for about half the cooking time. This produces a steady oven-type heat that's best for cooking the interior of thick steaks.

A long metal spatula is the ideal turning tool. If you develop an unusual sticking problem you can lick it by rubbing your spatula blade with cooking oil.

If you have favorite herbs you like to use in your cooking you can soak and drain some, then throw a few pinches on the coals just before you place your steaks on the hot grate. Smoldering herbs impart subtle flavors.

Beyond the simple generalities of grilling steaks you'll find that cooking fish on the grill is not a precise science. That's because no two grilling experts will agree on specific methods or cooking times. Two

---

IDEAS FOR MARINADES

Marinating fish steaks in a flavor-enhancing liquid is always a good way to preserve moisture during cooking. If you are in a real hurry to get cooking and have no marinade you can make do with a favorite liquid salad dressing from your refrigerator. If it tastes good on your salad it will work fine on your fish. Pour some into a glass bowl and marinate your steaks for 15 to 30 minutes. Italian salad dressing is one of the best.

If you have lots of time and want to try unusual marinades, here are three ideas to try. To one-half pound of butter or margarine (two sticks) and 2/3 cup white wine vinegar add:

1. One-quarter cup roasted red pepper... diced from cut rings. Plus two tablespoons minced green onion. Use both white and green parts.

2. Two tablespoons Dijon mustard plus two tablespoons minced onion.

3. One-quarter cup roasted garlic slivers plus two tablespoons chopped parsley.

Mix any one of these combinations thoroughly, heat and use to marinate. These proportions are enough for 8 to 10 salmon steaks.

---

opinions may vary dramatically, yet both may be correct. In many ways cooking fish is like filleting fish. Two expert filleters may use distinctly different cuts and still produce identical fillets.

Proper cooking times can vary according to many situations. Some grills cook a lot hotter than others. Some experts insist on grilling about four inches above the coals, others claim that closer to six inches is correct. Don't let such variables confuse you. Stick with the following basic fundamentals until you develop a system that cooks fish exactly the way you want it.

Most grilled fish cooks best over medium to medium-high heat. You'll know your heat is properly adjusted when you can hold your hand, palm down, about two inches above the cooking grate for at least two seconds before jerking it away.

Grilling times depend on the thickness of the fish pieces you're cooking. Thicker pieces take longer. The rule of thumb is that steaks or fillets should be at least 1-inch thick at the thickest part to be suitable for grilling. Thinner pieces turn out best when cooked with other methods.

Grilling baskets (the hinged wire type either oblong or rectangular) make turning delicate fillets a breeze. You'll save yourself a great deal of frustration by using a basket when grilling fillets from lean and tender species. Baskets are usually available where grilling accessories are sold. They rest on the grill and are easy to turn.

When you buy a new grill pay special attention to the grill racks. Fish tends to stick less to a heavy-metal grill grate than to the thinner, chrome-plated wire types.

Don't crowd pieces of fish on the grate. Leave plenty of extra space so you can move food around. There will be times when you'll want to move it out of range of flame or excess smoke.

If you use charcoal, always allow fumes from starter fluids to burn off before starting to cook.

When you marinate before cooking it's best to remove excess marinade by wiping your steaks or fillets with paper toweling. Wet fish meat is more likely to stick, and it will not crisp correctly. And, if it drips, it's likely to create smoke and flame.

Metal skewers provide an excellent anti-stick method for grilling fish. Make fish kebabs the same way you make beef kebabs, with chunks of meat about 1-inch square. Skewer the pieces of fish and prop them on a kebab rack so they're suspended about an inch above the cooking grate. The pieces of fish won't touch the grate so there's no way they can stick. Also, the kebabs are easy to turn.

One of the biggest cooking sins is to allow the very dry heat of grills to rob the fillets of moisture through overcooking. The best way to prevent this situation is to forget about grilling fillets less than 1-inch thick. Firm-fleshed and fattier species such salmon, lake trout, whitefish, and catfish are excellent candidates for grilling. Generally, the larger fish of any species produce the thickest and fattiest fillets.

But even thick fillets can be ruined quickly with excessive heat. No cooking method can overcook fish faster than grilling. For cooking average-size fillets on an open grill, place fish over hottest area of coals. Cook until edges of the fillets turn opaque, about 6 minutes. Turn fish over and cook 3 to 4 minutes longer. This is where inexperienced cooks err because they can't believe you can cook a 1-inch thick piece of meat in 10 minutes. Forever keep in mind that fish cooks fast, especially on an open grill.

It's a different story when using a covered grill. Now you should place fillets where they will not be directly over hot coals. Close cover and cook 8 to 10 minutes, then turn over and cook 6 to 7 minutes more. Remember, again, that grill cooking temperatures vary. These times are only guidelines. Experiment, and you'll find the right combinations of heat and cooking times.

A simple way to complement the naturally rich taste of grilled fish without masking its distinctive character is to flavor the fire with aromatic woods. Selected hardwoods such as red alder, apple, hickory—and certain regional varieties like mesquite—are available in ready-to-use chunks. Get them at cookware and hardware stores, and at home and garden centers. These wood chunks are especially effective with covered or kettle grills which hold in a bit of the smoke, thereby permeating the fish with flavor as it cooks.

One of the major tricks of the trade is remembering that thicker fillets must be placed further from the heat source than thin fillets. This is to ensure that the cooking process proceeds at more even temperatures. This in turn prevents the outside from cooking too fast and becoming overdone before the inside is ready. It's also important to avoid turning the fillets any more than you have to. It's best to fully cook one side of the fillet before turning it over. This principle applies to broiling and sauteing too. It gives you firmness in the fillet which reduces the chances of the tender meat breaking up when you flip it over.

Basting frequently while fish are grilling is another good technique because high temperatures and heat convection tend to dry out seafoods, especially leaner fish. As fish cook, the natural oils leach out. If you replace them with brushed-on seasoned marinades, butter, margarine or Italian salad dressing the flavors change for the better. The best solution is making enough marinade for tenderizing, and having enough left over for basting.

Here are the best grilling recipes I use. They're also the simplest and easiest to work with.

GRILLED SALMON STEAKS No.1

4 salmon steaks cut 1 to 1 1/4-inch thick
3 tablespoons melted margarine
1/2 teaspoon worchestershire sauce
2 teaspoons lemon juice

Mix last 3 ingredients. Brush mixture evenly on steaks while preheating grill to medium high. Grill first side 4 to 6 minutes or until crispy. Flip steaks and grill 3 to 4 minutes until done. This same dish is equally delicious when baked indoors during inclement weather. Grease shallow baking dish so steaks won't stick. Bake about 10 minutes in preheated 400 degree oven. Serves 4.

GRILLED SALMON STEAKS No. 2

4 salmon steaks cut 1 to 1 1/4-inch thick
3 tablespoons olive oil
2 tablespoons lemon juice
1 tablespoon soy sauce
1/2 teaspoon dry mustard

Combine and mix last 4 ingredients. Brush over steaks. Put in bowl. Cover with plastic wrap. Refrigerate for 1 hour, turning occasionally. Grill first side 4 to 6 minutes or until crispy. Flip steaks and grill 3 to 4 minutes until done. This recipe can also be baked as described in above recipe. Serves 4.

GRILLED WALLEYE

4 6-ounce pieces of walleye fillets
1/4 cup olive oil
1/2 cup white wine

2 heaping tablespoons green onions minced
1 tablespoon dill minced
Seasonings to taste

Combine and mix last 5 ingredients. Brush over fillets. Put in bowl. Marinate 1 hour. Pat meat dry with paper toweling. Grill first side 5 minutes or until crispy. Turn and grill second side 4 minutes. Serves 4.

GRILLED SMALL, WHOLE WALLEYE

2 small walleyes (about 16 inches in the one to 2 1/2-pound range) and gutted with heads removed.
1/4 cup dry sherry or white wine
1/4 cup olive oil
Juice of two limes
Several sprigs fresh rosemary or 1 tablespoon dried
Several lemon wedges

Mix together wine, olive oil and juice. Brush onto fish while grill is preheating to medium-hot. When ready to cook sprinkle a bit of rosemary on the fish, then place on the grill. Cook about 5 to 8 minutes per side, basting occasionally with remaining marinade. Check for doneness by peering into cut made along backbone with tip of fillet knife blade. The fish is done when the meat along the cut is white and flaky. Garnish with rosemary sprigs and lemon wedges. Serves 2 to 3. Double or triple the ingredients for more servings.

This is a really neat recipe for almost any small fish that is big enough to grill. Walleyes work particularly well because their skin is tasty and crisps well. It works great with big crappies, too. Other good bets are smallmouth bass and salt water spotted sea trout. I used this recipe last winter on some of these trout. They were magnificent. Years ago I noted a similar recipe that called for small whole salt water bluefish, pompano, mackerel, or red snapper. I got my recipe from a Kentucky angler who told me that white bass cooked this way make a fish dinner as succulent as it can get. I don't normally want to cook fish containing bones, but this is an exception. The recipe also allows you to grill fish that are too small for grilling in fillet form. Also, the skeletons provide stability.

Still, one of my favorite recipes is for salmon grilled in foil. It's a technique my wife refers to as "Fish on the lettuce leaf."

Tear off a sheet of foil large enough to wrap around your salmon fillet. In middle of foil fashion a bed of thin lettuce leaves just wide enough to nestle your meat. Spread a thin coating of mayonnaise over entire fillet. Season lightly with Lawry's seasoned salt and a sprinkling of paprika. Lay fillet on lettuce, barely cover it with another very thin layer of lettuce leaves, then wrap loose ends of foil around all ingredients and seal package. Cook over indirect heat of preheated medium-hot grill for about 15 minutes.

BEST FISH FOR GRILLING

The most important thought to keep in mind about grilling unwrapped fish fillets is that some species are made to order for grilling and some aren't. If ever a fish was meant to be grilled, it is tuna. If ever a fish was designed to appeal to beef lovers, it is a thick tuna steak rubbed with olive oil and grilled medium rare in exactly the same way a prime T-bone is cooked, except faster.

Other salt water species producing thick, firm steaks ideal for unwrapped grilling include grouper, mahi-mahi and swordfish. Salmon, lake trout, and steelhead head the list for freshwaters species Leaner, softer-fleshed species are grilled best when enclosed in wire baskets or wrapped in foil.

Open grill cover to check progress. Unwrap foil and open top of package. At this point the edges of lettuce should be turning a cooked brown. Leave package open, close cover and cook another 10 minutes. (Note: These cooking times are longer than normal because you're cooking in an insulated package plus the lettuce, which provides unique flavor and prevents fish from sticking to foil.) Remove fillet to warming plate and cut into serving-size pieces. Edge food with sprigs of parsley and lemon wedges. Now you have a salmon dinner that's a unique treat, a meal you'll want to cook over and over.

If you don't like mayonnaise substitute Dijon mustard. Spread a thin coating evenly over entire unmarinated fillet. Or, you might prefer a crisp crusting of fresh minced herbs. Make any combination of parsley, chives, basil, sage, thyme or rosemary. Mix with two tablespoons olive oil. Rub

0

on fillet and grill as directed above.

The same recipes work great with walleye fillets too, except it's best to add 4 tablespoons of water. This will produce more steam which helps to keep the dryer walleye meat moist.

Foil also is the way to go when cooking fish with fresh vegetables. The fresher the fish and the fresher the vegetables the better the meal. Try this goodie.

1-2 lbs. boneless fish fillets
Garlic salt
1/4 stick butter
1 lb. broccoli
1/4 lb. asparagus tops
1 whole onion, thinly sliced
1-2 small zucchini, thinly sliced
1 lb. fresh mushrooms, sliced
Grated Parmesan cheese

Prepare four squares of aluminum foil - 16 to 18 inches square. Grease centers with a little soft butter. Sprinkle butter with garlic salt to taste. After rinsing fillets in cold water, arrange equal portions in the center of each foil square. Large fillets may be cut into chunks for better cooking. Divide vegetables equally and place atop each portion of fish. Sprinkle each again lightly with garlic salt. Then sprinkle each portion with Parmesan cheese and 1 tbsp. cold water. Seal fish and vegetables inside each foil square by forming a pouch, leaving a little room for expansion during cooking. Place packets, fish side down, directly on hot grill and cook for 7-10 minutes. Flip packets and cook another 7 to 10 minutes. Open and serve hot. Serves 4.

I wrote down the above recipe while sitting in a North Dakota duck blind in a fog so thick we couldn't see a duck if one did fly by. To pass the time Dave Austin and I talked about the state's famous walleye fishing and how to cook the catch.

"Fresh is best by far," said Dave. "That's why I have a big garden. When the walleye bite is on in Lake Sakakawea I can often catch as many walleye as I want. I release everything except the last two I boat. Then I hurry home, fillet 'em out, and go pick fresh vegetables in the garden.

What isn't growing fresh at the moment I get out of my freezer. I freeze my own stuff whenever it's in season.

"Maybe we better go fishing tomorrow morning instead of duck hunting. I'll cook dinner with the recipe I just gave you. You'll never sit down to a better meal of walleyes. The man who has access to fresh fish fillets and just picked vegetables from his own garden lives like a king."

Here's one more recipe emphasizing the importance of fresh vegetables.

GRILLED WALLEYE WITH CORN & TOMATO RELISH

4 small walleye fillets (or 2 big ones cut into 4 pieces about 6 ounces each)
3 tablespoons olive oil
4 ears fresh corn, stripped of kernels
2 large fresh ripe tomatoes, cored and roughly chopped
1/8 cup minced fresh basil

Note: If you live in northern states make this dish only in late summer. Without ultra fresh corn and tomatoes it's pointless. If you fish in the south during winter you can pick these vegetables fresh at U-Pick stands. The recipe works great with saltwater fish such as snappers, sea trout, redfish and snook.

Preheat grill while brushing the fillets with half the olive oil. Season as desired. Heat a small skillet and cook corn in remaining oil until lightly browned, about 2 minutes. Add tomato and basil. Cook 30 seconds more, then turn off heat. Grill the fish in a basket about 3 inches above medium high heat until nicely browned, about 4 or 5 minutes. Turn and cook about 3 more minutes. Serve on heated plates with the relish. Serves 4.

The most important grilling secret involving salmon, steelhead and other large trout is the huge advantage of skin-on cooking. Because the skin is oily it practically guarantees non-stick grilling. The skin (scales on) also holds the juices in and the meat together.

The lone disadvantage of this technique is that you can't remove the dark strip of fat along the lateral line of the fish before cooking. One way to lick this problem is to slide the meat off the skin during the last minute or so of grilling. By this time the flesh and skin is firm and will separate easily. You can also serve the fish with the skin on, then separate the good meat from the bad stuff with the edge of a fork. This is easy to do when the flesh is hot.

You can grill skin-on lean fish with this same technique, but the pieces will stick to hot grates unless brushed frequently with marinade or cooking oil. Rule of thumb for all 3-inch-wide chunks of fillets: grill skin side down for 6 minutes, then flip and cook 4 more minutes.

The second big consideration with grilling or broiling lean fish is their natural mild taste. Fillets from oily species have a built-in flavor that's missing from such species as walleye or bass. Marinades help solve the twin problems of sticking and lack of taste. The simplest marinade I use is a mixture of two-thirds butter and one-third lemon juice. This combination tends to firm up the meat as it cooks, in addition to adding taste.

When you grill this way you are subjecting your fillet to almost the same cooking process as sauteing. Think about this for a minute, using lake perch as an example. Have you ever heard of anybody grilling or broiling perch? Probably not, because pan frying is the accepted best technique. A walleye belongs to the same fish family as perch. It tastes about the same as perch but is big enough to grill. I've found that I can add various tastes to grilled walleye by utilizing rubs or marinades. Lawry's Herb & Garlic marinade is one of my favorites. (See chapter 10 for much more on this subject.)

Lean fish are made to order for grilling in fish baskets. A basket solves the problem of lean flesh sticking to hot grates.

Don't even think of freezing skin-on oily fish for use months later. If you do this you're freezing the fat along the lateral line. This fat begins turning rancid within weeks of being frozen. If you grill this stuff in your garage during winter you will stink up your place something terrible. I know because I learned the hard way.

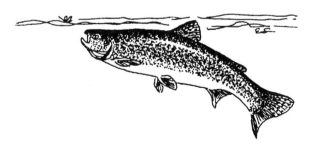

Broiling
Techniques

There are four basic differences between grilling and broiling.

1. The position of the heat source: In grilling it is below the food. In broiling it's above.

2. The fuel for the heat source: In grilling it may be wood, charcoal, briquets, or gas. In broiling it's either electricity or gas.

3. The flavor: In grilling it's determined primarily by the fuel and what's placed on top of it. Wood-grilled food has a distinctive flavor that's almost always enjoyed by everyone. Charcoal fires and gas-grill briquets produce a flavor that can be helped along by the addition of herbs or special wood chips. The flavors of broiled fish can usually be helped only with the use of marinades.

4. The location of your cooking units: Broilers are almost always inside, and grills outside. This tends to associate broiled fish with winter or other inclement weather rather than summer or other pleasant weather. This, of course, isn't always true. Dedicated fish cooks like myself use their outside grills almost year around. Some variety in cooking methods always offers a change in pace. Although nobody wants to make a summer-hot kitchen even hotter by turning on the stove, most fish can be broiled in 10 minutes. The accumulated heat is rarely a problem.

One of the major advantages of broiling is that it's less fussy than grilling. And, because it's usually easier to adjust the distance from the heat source to the food, it gives you greater control. This is important if you want to cook thin panfish fillets. You can broil them two inches from the heat source, getting them browned before they overcook. That's hard to do on a grill, and it's one reason why most experts recommend that fillets should be at least 1-inch thick at their thickest part for proper grilling.

The key to successful broiling is the same in grilling...ALWAYS PREHEAT your cooking unit. A big advantage with broiling is that you usually don't have to bother with turning the fish. The ambient temperature is high enough so that the bottom and the interior cook as the top browns. Most experts turn only the thickest fillets and, of course, whole fish.

Then there's the simplicity of broiling. You can cut a fillet off a fish, wash it and wipe it nearly dry with paper toweling, brush it with olive oil and put it in the broiler. About 10 minutes later your fillet is ready for the table. Using marinades for flavor doesn't take much longer. Serve with parsley sprigs and lemon wedges for added flavor. No cooking process can produce a quality meal much faster, and you can use your seasonings of choice either during or after cooking.

Fish can be placed 2 to 6 inches from the heat. The thinner the fillet the closer it should be. This means that those thin panfish fillets are ideal for broiling, which further means you can eliminate the fat required in frying. Typically, thin panfish fillets can be broiled in 3 to 4 minutes. Further, since most broiled fish doesn't have to be turned, the risk of breaking those little fillets is much diminished.

There's also the great advantage of almost instant temperature control in broiling. If the top of your fish is browning too fast you can simply turn down the oven temperature. This stops the browning process but continues cooking the fish by baking, thereby eliminating the necessity of turning the fillet. You also achieve the goal of a nicely browned top simultaneously with a cooked interior.

Doneness with broiling is a matter of taste just as it is with any other cooking method. To me, broiled fish should be cooked through. Many cooking experts claim that if you cook fish until it is completely opaque throughout it's overcooked and you're going to be eating dry fish. Julia Childs goes so far as to say that if fish is cooked this much it's ruined. Many cooks want their fish fairly rare, but I just don't buy this approach. To me, under cooked fish on the rare side is unsavory to say the least. It's almost as bad a biting into bones in a fillet that's supposed to be bone free.

I like my fish cooked firm enough to eliminate any suggestion of raw or slimy meat. This is the difficult part of broiling because the high-heat process tends to dry out fish. Consider that you're trying to get the interior of your fillet to about 125 degrees (cooked properly) in an oven that's about 400 degrees. The best solution to the dryness problem with lean fish is basting with marinades, cooking oils, margarine, vegetables or anything else that replaces the moisture that evaporates during the broiling process.

Two of my best broiling recipes contain moisture holding vegetables.

BROILED BLUEGILLS...OR OTHER PANFISH

2 pounds panfish fillets
1/2 cup unpeeled cucumber, chopped
1/4 cup Helman's light mayonnaise
1 teaspoon dried dill or 1 tablespoon minced fresh dill
3 green onions, chopped
1/2 teaspoon lemon juice
4 drops Tabasco sauce
Lemon wedges

Spray cooking oil on broiling pan. Arrange fillets in single layer in pan. Combine the rest of the ingredients and spread evenly over fillets. Broil in preheated 400 degree oven, 4 inches from heat for 4 to 5 minutes until tops of fillets are browned and bubbly. They'll be bubbly from the moisture cooking out of the vegetables. Serve with lemon wedges. Serves 4.

BROILED WALLEYE FILLETS ON SPINACH BED

This one came from a grouse hunting and walleye addict I fished with in Minnesota. He had a big garden behind his house. Several rows of spinach flourished in that garden, and I found out why after we returned from a few hours of walleye fishing.

2 medium to large walleye fillets (skinned)
1/4 teaspoon seasoned salt
1/4 cup melted margarine or butter
1/4 teaspoon dried dill weed
1/4 teaspoon onion powder (or garlic powder)
1 large colander rinsed spinach leaves with tough stems removed.
Put in boiling water and simmer while preparing fish as follows.

Set oven control to broil. Grease or spray broiler pan, place in oven to preheat. If walleye fillets are large, cut into 8 serving pieces; otherwise 6. Sprinkle both sides with seasoned salt (also 1/8 teaspoon pepper if desired). Place in broiler pan. Mix remaining ingredients except spinach. Brush on fillets. Broil with tops of fillets 4 inches from heat source for 4 or 5 minutes. Drain and butter cooked spinach and make beds of spinach on warm serving plates. Place walleye fillets on spinach beds. Let fish remain on hot spinach for 3 to 4 minutes to soak up moisture. Then eat while combination is still warm. Add squeezed lemon or lime juice for more moisture and flavoring if desired. I don't have to tell you to remember this recipe. If you do it right you'll never forget the magnificent flavors each time you prepare this dish.

HERBED BROILED BASS

2 pounds bass fillets
1/2 teaspoon seasoned salt
1/4 cup margarine or butter, softened
1/4 teaspoon dried dill weed
1/8 teaspoon dried thyme leaves
1/8 teaspoon onion powder

Set oven control to broil. Grease broiler pan and place in oven to preheat. Cut fillets into 8 serving pieces. Sprinkle both sides with seasoned salt (and pepper if desired). Place fillets in broiler pan. Mix remaining ingredients and brush light coating over fillets.

Broil with tops 4 inches from heat source for 6 to 8 minutes or until light brown. Brush fillets with part of remaining mixture. Turn carefully and brush with remaining margarine mixture. Broil 5 minutes longer or until fish flakes easily with fork. Bass is lean meat that dries out quickly without the brushing of margarine mixture, thus the called for 1/4 cup is correct. If you try to make do with less margarine your bass will be too dry, a common problem with broiled bass. Even with this amount of margarine the cholesterol count per serving is only 35 mg.

BROILED BASS No. 2

1/2 teaspoon seasoned salt
2 tablespoons lemon juice
2 egg whites...beaten stiff
1 1/2 tablespoon Dijon mustard
2 tablespoons chopped green onions (both green and whites)
2 bass fillets cut into 4 servings

Set oven control to broil. Spray broiler pan with nonstick cooking spray. Sprinkle fillet pieces with seasoned salt and place in broiler pan. Brush fish with half of lemon juice. Broil with tops 4 inches from heat source for about 5 minutes or until light brown. Turn and brush with remaining lemon juice. Broil 2 minutes longer. Slide broiler pan out of oven and onto opened door. Fold beaten egg whites in mustard and onion. Spread mixture over fish and broil about 2 minutes or until topping is golden brown. The cholesterol in this recipe goes up to 50 mg per serving, but the egg-mustard-mixture adds a unque flavor and moisture.

The trick in broiling all lean fish is to remember that you're cooking at very high temperatures (about 500 degrees just under the flame or broiler coil). Intense heat evaporates moisture in a hurry, so basting and/ or topping fillets with moisture producing additions is a must. A good trick is to top each fillet with very thin slices of lemon or cucumber. Dabbing frequently with a herb-butter mixture also helps. You can lend a nice color to all broiled fish by sprinkling paprika on each fillet before cooking.

More broiling tips: Generally, when the top of the fish is nicely golden crisp, the meat is cooked through. Even if you use lemon juice or lemon slices in the broiling process it's still a good idea to serve broiled fish with lemon wedges. They add color plus adding moisture with a quick squeeze. Sprigs of fresh green parsley always add needed color to broiled fish.

BROILED BASS No. 3

2 tablespoons vegetable oil
1 clove garlic, cut in half

1/2 cup white wine
1/4 teaspoon cyenne pepper
1 teaspoon minced garlic
1 tablespoon minced green onion, both parts
Bass fillets cut into 6 serving pieces

Preheat broiler. Rub fish pieces with the oil, then with the cut sides of the garlic. Season to taste. Place evenly in nonstick broiler pan, and put into oven about 4 inches from heat source. Broil until the flesh turns white, about 4 to 6 minutes.

Remove fish and put on warm serving platter. Simmer the remaining ingredients for 2 minutes. Pour, hot, over the bass pieces. Now you have broiled fish with pleanty of moisture. You can simmer a substitute mixture consisting of 1 tablespoon horseradish, 1/2 cup rice vinegar, and 1/4 cup minced green onion. If you don't like horseradish, try 1 1/2 tablespoons soy sauce. My wife hates horseradish, but thinks this recipe is fine with soy sauce. These recipes work great with any lean-fish fillets.

This book would never have seen print if it wasn't for the encouragement of Dave Richey, outdoor writer for The Detroit News. Said Dave, "You ought to include a real simple broiling recipe, one that anybody can use on the spur of the moment. I've got one for any oily-meated fish that you can broil without marinating. I use it for whitefish.

"Place whitefish fillets in broiling pan. Sprinkle lightly with salt and lemon pepper. Broil until half done. Turn fillets and squeeze 1/2 fresh lemon over each fillet. Sprinkle with paprika for color. Broil again until done. That's all there is to it."

Thanks Dave. My basic recipe for broiling lean fish isn't much more work. I mentioned it in Chapter 6, but here it is again. Make a marinade of one-third lemon juice to two-thirds margarine. Brush both sides of fillets with this heated mixture, marinate for half an hour, then broil in preheated oven.

Here are a few broiling tips that will help when broiling with any recipe.

1. Always broil lean fish at a greater distannce from the heat souce than oily fish because they cook faster.

2. Always preheat your oven. It's best to preheat your broiling pan too. This helps to cook the bottoms of your fillets which are the farthest from the heat source.

3. Basting lean fish throughout the cooking time helps seal in natural moisture and keeps the meat from drying out.

4. It's best to avoid broiling thick cuts or whole fish because the outside portions become dry and leathery before the inside portions get cooked. Such cuts are much better baked, or close-cover grilled, which is a form of baking. The only differences between baking and broiling are the source of the heat and the cooking times. To me, broiling is a much better technique.

5. Broiled lean fish lacks in appetizing color. For toppings with color consider fresh mint, chopped black olives or red pepper flakes. If you want more exotic toppings try sliced almonds or maraschino cherries. All of these items add color and flavor.

6. Be cautious with soy, terriyake, worchestershire or Cajum marinades. If left on fish too long, the high salt contents will draw out moisture, leaving the fish tough and dry. This is exactly opposite of what you want to happen. Don't leave these marinades on lean fillets more than half an hour before broiling them. An excellent substitute offering sharp taste without the problems is garlic butter used for marinating and basting.

7. Broiling is one of the easiest ways to cook perfect fish dinners, if you stay close to the action and guard against overcooking.

8. Simple rule of thumb for broiling most fish: Place broiler rack 4 inches under heat source, preheat oven for 4 or 5 minutes, broil fillets in the 1-inch thick bracket for 8 to 10 minutes, remove and eat.

9. You can make your own garlic butter marinade and basting as follows:

> 1/4 teaspoon garlic salt
> 1 tablespoon minced garlic
> Lemon-pepper seasoning
> 1/2 stick butter (not margarine)

In a small frying pan over medium-low heat combine all ingredients. Heat 3 to 5 minutes to release the flavor of the garlic into the butter, taking care that the mixture does not burn. Remove from heat and set aside.

Top Tips

For

Cooking Ocean Fish

No matter what you do in life there are always some people who can do it better. I often meet chefs who have much more cooking experience than I do. I marvel at their abilities. Professional cooks who prepare fish every day are the experts who are loaded with knowledge. The problem is that many of these pros refuse to divulge their cooking secrets. They want to keep their best methods to themselves. Their livelihood depends on remaining tops in their profession.

So it came as a great surprise when I discovered a combination fish market and white-tablecloth restaurant called the Prawnbroker in Ft. Myers, Florida. There are branches in Stuart, Sanibel Island and Port Salemo, FL. In short, this organization has many chefs cooking fish seven days a week. Do they keep their secrets from the public? Not by a long shot.

"We brag about our fish knowledge and recipes," says Steve Wolfe, general manager. "We have a rack on the wall holding printouts of some of our best recipes. Anyone who buys fish or eats here is welcome to take copies of whatever fish-cooking information they want. Besides the recipes you'll find some great tips. Incidentally, all our fish is personally selected by one of the owners and filleted on the premises."

The rest of this chapter contains the best information I found in those printouts.

EVERYTHING YOU WANTED TO KNOW ABOUT BAKED FISH AND WEREN'T AFRAID TO ASK!

A. PREHEAT OVEN TO 450 DEGREES
B. PLACE FILLETS IN GREASED BAKING DISH
C. ADD WATER (OR WINE) 1/4-INCH HIGH IN DISH
D. ADD SEASONINGS (Lemon, butter, salt, pepper, etc.)
E. COOK ABOUT 10 MINUTES PER INCH THICKNESS OF FILLET

WHY DO WE SUGGEST THIS METHOD?

1. The fish should be put in a hot oven to cook properly and evenly.

2. The dish should be greased to prevent the fish from sticking to it.

3. ADDING WATER: This is the most important factor in the way we cook fish. When the baking dish is placed in the hot oven, the water (or wine) will heat up and eventually turn to steam. This will turn your "dry oven" into a "moist oven." The steam will protect the fish, and prevent it from drying out. The natural juices and moisture in the fish (which gives the fish it's distinct flavor) will remain.

4. Adding seasoning is a matter of taste. Depending on the fish and your personal preferences, it can be as simple as lemon and pepper or more exotic such as fresh vegetables or seasoned mayonnaise.

5. The "basic timing" rule of cooking fish is 10 minutes per inch. As oven temperatures vary, cooking times may vary. The type of fish may also affect cooking times (some fish are denser than others and will take more time). As with cooking any seafood, most importantly:

DO NOT OVERCOOK THE FISH

To check to see if the fish is done, poke it with a fork so that you can see inside the fillet. UNCOOKED FISH IS TRANSLUCENT (CLEAR). If your fish is still clear in the center put it back in the oven for a minute. COOKED FISH IS OPAQUE (white). If the fish is opaque, serve it! Remember, it is always better to take the fish out too soon, as you can always cook it more, but there is no way of "un-cooking" it. (If you know of a process for "un-cooking" fish, please get in touch with me immediately as we can both make a lot of money!) Bon Appetite! ... The Fishmonger

DOLPHIN

A cause for much misunderstanding is the FISH known as the Dolphin. It is commonly confused with the MAMMAL also known as dolphin or porpoise. The MAMMAL dolphin is in the family *Delpinidae* which belongs to the order of whales. This is the animal most of us recognize as "Flipper." It is not eaten.

The FISH dolphin, however, is one of the most delicious seafood around. The meat is unique, large flaked, and sweetly moist. It is common in the Atlantic from the Carolina's to South America. The largest Dolphin fleets are in Hawaii, where the Dolphin is known as MAHI - MAHI. Many restaurants use the name of Mahi - Mahi when serving dolphin to avoid the confusion of "eating "Flipper." However, at The Prawnbroker, we serve locally caught dolphin (it is plentiful throughout the Keys and off the East Coast), and, therefore, sell it as Dolphin, not Mahi - Mahi or Dorado (the Mexican name for Dolphin).

Dolphin fish range in size from 3 - 5 pounds (schoolies) up to 50 - 60 pounds (bulls). The larger male is distinguished from the female by an almost vertical, squared off head profile. When caught, the fish display an ever changing rainbow of bright blues, greens, and yellow, which fade away as the fish dies.

COOKING - Dolphin is a very versatile fish that lends itself to cooking in almost any fashion. Even when skinned, the firm meat will stay intact when tossed on a grill. The slightly colored meat turns white as the fish cooks. For this reason, we suggest charcoal grilling a dolphin. That is how we serve it!

CHAR-BROILED DOLPHIN A LA TIMBERS WEST

4 - 8 Oz. Dolphin Fillet
1/4 cup soy sauce
1/2 cup orange juice
1/2 cup melted butter

Mix the soy sauce, orange juice and melted butter thoroughly. Dip the Dolphin fillets in the mixture and then immediately place on the hot grill. BE CAREFUL AS THIS MIXTURE WILL CAUSE THE GRILL TO

FLARE! Cook about 3-4 minutes, baste with the marinade, then turn and baste again. THE EXACT COOKING TIME WILL DEPEND ON THE THICKNESS OF THE DOLPHIN AND THE HEAT OF THE GRILL. As with all fish ... DO NOT OVERCOOK!

RED SNAPPER

Description: Moist sweet white flesh, probably the most popular of all Florida fishes, sweeter and more tender than grouper.

Snappers are one of the most important fish families (*Lutjanidae*) of the tropical seas. While there is only one true species known as Red Snapper (Lutjanus Campechanus), many other Snappers, as well as some other species of fish, are passed off as Red Snapper.

When filleted and skinned before cooking, the taste and texture of these fish are hard to differentiate from genuine American Red Snapper. That is why we buy all of our Snappers whole, so that we know what we are buying. As with Grouper, the size of the fish (which determines the size of the fillet), is very important.

A 2-pound red snapper will have more similar characteristics to a 2-pound lane snapper than it will to a 20-pound red snapper. Hog snapper, silver snapper and yellowtail snapper, while being premium table fish, are not in the true snapper family. All three fish are highly recommended as a substitute for, or as a change from red snapper. All are equally suitable for sauteing, baking, broiling or poaching.

SNAPPER ALMONDINE (Serves four)

Four 7 - 8 oz. Snapper fillets
1/2 cup silvered almonds
1/2 cup flour
1/4 dry white wine
1/4 cup olive oil
Juice of a small lemon
Salt and pepper to taste
2 Tbls. chopped parsley

1. Pat fillets dry and sprinkle with salt, pepper and lemon juice

2. Coat the fillets with the flour on both sides

3. Saute in heated oil about 4 -5 minutes each side. (Actual cooking

time will depend on the thickness of the fish and temperature of the oil.) Remove to heated serving dish.

4. Add the almonds to the remaining oil and saute until golden. Add white wine and reduce.

5. Pour the almonds and wine mixture over the Snapper fillets and garnish with chopped parsley.

6. If you burn it, undercook it or it doesn't taste good, have dinner with us!

GROUPER

Description: Very firm white flesh with a mild flavor. Milder than snapper, but not quite as moist or tender.

Groupers are members of the sea bass family Serranidae, which is composed of over 400 species. Culinary speaking, only the species Epinephelus and Mycteroperca are important. Some of the better groupers of these species that have appeared on our menu include:

Black Grouper, Gag Grouper, Tiger and Yellowfin Grouper.

It is very hard to note the differences in the taste or texture of these different groupers, as they are all white fleshed and lean. The skin is tough, so the fish does not lend itself to cooking whole or as an unskinned fillet. The most important factor in buying and cooking grouper is the SIZE of the natural fillet. As fish grow older and larger, their flesh gets tougher and less flavorful. Giant grouper (300 - 750 lbs.), such as the Jewfish and Warsaw Grouper usually end up in chowder. Large groupers (25 -50 lbs.) lend themselves best to being cut into fingers and fried. The smaller groupers (2 - 20 lbs.) which are the type we try to buy are equally at home in the broiler, or fryer.

CRUNCHY GROUPER (Serves four)

Four 7 -8 oz. Grouper fillets
1/2 cup flavored bread crumbs
1/2 cup Special K cereal
1/2 cup corn flakes
1 cup vegetable oil
2 eggs
1/2 cup milk

1. Mix bread crumbs, Special K and corn flakes together

2. Whisk milk and eggs together well

3. Dredge grouper fillets through milk/egg mixture and then coat with cereal mixture (you may need to press the cereal against the grouper)

4. Saute in heated oil about 4 - 5 minutes each side. (actual cooking time will depend on the thickness of the fish and the temperature of the oil)

SWORDFISH

The swordfish is found in all temperate waters of the world, with a large concentration off the Atlantic Coast from Canada to the Gulf of Mexico. In the fall and winter, they prefer the more Southern Atlantic, while migrating to the North in the spring and summer.

The meat of the Swordfish is quite hard to describe as it is unique in flavor and texture. Only the Mako and Thresher sharks taste similar to Swordfish.

Most important to the retail consumer is the size of the fish your steak has been cut from. Swordfish range in size from 25 - 250 pounds, with all sizes entering the wholesale market. As it is also important to get a steak from 3/4 to 1-1/4 inch thick, the size of the fish will determine whether you're getting a half quarter, or "slice" of the Swordfish. The larger the fish, the smaller the "slice" of the pie.

When looking at the Swordfish steak, you should look at the color and shine on the fish. The flesh should be shiny, almost translucent with the bloodline being a red or pink color. An older fish or one that has been frozen will have a dull "soggy" looking flesh and the blood line will be a dark brown.

Aside from the spinal column, the Swordfish has no other bones, making it a favorite of diners. The belly meat is considered a delicacy in many parts of the world because it is sweet and tender. The Swordfish may be baked, broiled, or fried, but it's firm steak-like texture lends itself best to charcoal grilling. Just be sure to wipe the steaks with some sort of shortening or marinade to prevent it from sticking to the grill.

YELLOWFIN TUNA - Thunnus Albacares

The Yellowfin Tuna is just one of several species of Tuna, all of which are part of the Mackerel family. Other popular species of Tuna include the Albacore, Bigeye Tuna, Blackfin Tuna, Bluefin Tuna, Little Tunas and Skipjack Tuna. Yellowfin Tuna are found in tropical and sub-tropical waters around the world, as well as in the gulf stream as far north as New Jersey (although the majority of Tuna caught in New England is Bluefin). The average weight of Tuna that reaches the market is between 25 - 125 lbs. although it is thought that some fish may possibly reach 400 lbs.

BUYING FRESH TUNA: There are two main considerations when buying Tuna at the market. These considerations apply to all "steak fish."

1. Freshness: Think of Tuna as a New York Strip Steak when you are in the market. It should have a bright red color and a translucent sheen to it. As the Tuna gets older, the color will turn to brown and then grayish, and the sheen will be dull. What was once firm flesh, will become soft and mushy.

2. Thickness: Again, think of the Tuna as a beef steak. A prime N.Y. strip that is cut 1/4 to 1/2 inch in thickness will not have the flavor, juiciness and texture of that same steak if it has been cut 1 to 1 1/4 inches of thickness. If you enjoy biting into a nice thick steak, ask for a thick cut of Tuna. Properly cooked, it is magnificent!

EATING FRESH TUNA: Don't forget the steak! Just as with beef, fresh tuna may be eaten raw (*sashimi and sushi*), cooked medium rare or cooked thoroughly in any variety of ways. It's firm texture makes it a great fish to charcoal grill as well as using Tuna chunks for kabobs.

As a rule, you will do well to cook your tuna steak as you would a strip steak on the grill. If you like your steak rare, cook your tuna the same way with a bright red center. If you like your steak medium, cook your tuna until it's pink in the center. TRY IT - YOU'LL LIKE IT. You can always throw it back on the grill to cook it a little more, but trust me...you won't!"

This is probably the place to say more about eating raw fish called sushi. I certainly can't recommend it because I've never tried it. The preparation of this dish is the most difficult fish meal I've ever heard of. Be glad you don't have to learn the complicated tricks of this trade.

Sushi lovers in the USA think they get good stuff at their favorite spots, but it can't compare with the real thing made in Japan. Hisao

Ohuchi, now in his 70s, has been a chef all his life. He spent a decade in training before he was even allowed to make sushi. First he worked, watched and observed at restaurants in Tokyo before returning to his home city of Nagano. There he apprenticed for 20 years before opening his own eatery.

"From the start I wanted to be a sushi chef." he says. "I've always focused on sushi. It is my life! In Japan, those who want to master sushi must work their way up. Other chefs won't tell you how to do it. You have to observe to learn. My father taught me, and I have taught my son so he can carry on the tradition. I've too old now to handle all the necessary work involved myself. We both do our jobs without overburdening each other."

All that sounds to me like it's far too much work for preparing a single meal of fish. I'll stick with the simple ways.

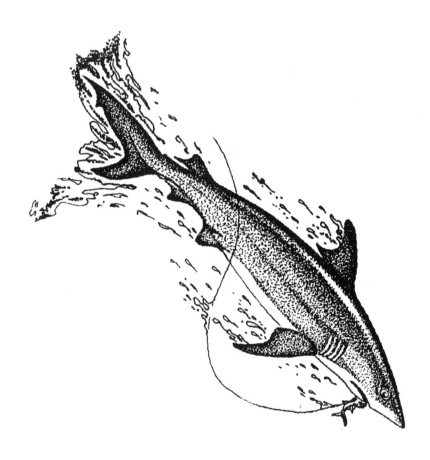

Rubs and Marinades

The fat content of top quality fish largely determines its flavor. Fatty fish with a higher proportion of oil tend to be more distinctly flavored than lean fish, which are milder and more delicate in flavor. For means of comparison, consider the difference between a venison round steak which has practically no fat and a well marbled T-bone beef steak. The T-bone will taste richer with distinctive flavor because fat contains much of the taste of meat. The same is true with fish. So, in cooking, you should choose the seasonings that best complement the flavor and fat content of your fish. (See chart on page 62.)

In general, the stronger-flavored fatty fish are best cooked in dry heat — broiled, grilled, baked or smoked — because their internal fat keeps them moist while they cook. Lean fish, because they have only a small amount of internal fat, are best cooked in moist heat. The appropriate methods are poaching, braising, steaming, frying (sauteing) and deep frying. Lean fish can also be cooked in dry heat if marinated, basted during cooking, or covered by a vegetable mixture.

Fatty fish (salmon, lake trout, steelhead and whitefish for example) all stand up well to strong seasonings such as mustard, citrus juices, red wine, soy sauce, horseradish, vinegars, olive oils and paprika.

The most delicate-tasting lean fish (such as walleye, northern pike,

91

bass and panfish) are better complimented with all kinds of herbs, many vegetables and mild cheeses such as Swiss and Parmesan. All of the onion family and all citrus juices also go well with lean fish.

The quickest and easiest way to add flavor to fish is to use a rub. A rub is no more than a mixture of herbs and spices patted to the surface of meat or fish. Rubs add instant flavor but do not tenderize, therefore they're great for all fish that don't need tenderizing. Rubs have no added fat and virtually no calories. There are no rules about flavor combinations or amounts of ingredients. Rubs let you be both casual and creative. They're quick and forgiving so use whatever ingredients you know and like. With a bit of experimentation you'll hit on combinations that are special for some of your fish dinners. Here's one that works great with fatty fish.

> 2 tablespoons Dijon mustard
> 1 tablespoon olive oil
> 1/4 teaspoon paprika
> citrus juice of your preference
> salt-free garlic and herb seasoning to taste

Make a paste and rub over enough fillets to serve 2. Grill or broil.

Here's an idea for lean fish.

> 2 tablespoons lemon juice
> 2 tablespoons chopped fresh parsley
> 1 tablespoon chopped fresh chives
> 2 tablespoon chopped green onions
> salt-free garlic and herb seasoning to taste

Mix together and pat onto 12 large panfish fillets just after dusting with flour. Saute immediately. Serves 4. (Tip: You can also mix ingredients on a large paper plate, then press fillets against them.)

Rubs also play a part in the cooking of large fish and fish of less than top quality, specifically freshwater species taken from warm, summer waters. I wouldn't think of using rubs on walleyes in the 2-pound class taken from cold May waters. I strongly believe in leaving good fish pretty much alone because their natural taste can't be beat. But it's a different story with lunkers weighing 5-pounds or more. Taste quality diminishes rapidly in older fish. Some species are worse than others. A 5-pound largemouth bass taken from a warm summer slough is almost inedible without flavor-enhancing rubs or marinades.

Marinades are the way to go when tenderness is the goal. The trick with all such accompaniments is not to overwhelm the main ingredient, but to complement it and bring out the original flavor. Consider that a lunker bass fillet may be tough and a bit muddy tasting without a marinade, but you can bring some flavor out with proper seasonings.

Oil-based marinades are especially good for enhancing the flavors of dry-textured fish. Those blending acid-flavored liquids (wine, vinegar and citrus juices) with spices, herbs and seasonings such as garlic and onions always bring out flavor. You can prepare such marinades with a lot of chopping, grinding and crushing of seasonings, then blending the works in a food processor. I consider all this work an enormous waste of time. You can buy ready-to-use liquid marinades in any good supermarket. Select the flavors you want to use and you're in business.

There are tricks of the trade that will help you achieve top marinating results. Select a snug container that allows your marinade to cover the fillets. Use plastic or glass containers because the acids and alcohol in marinades can react with aluminum or iron, giving fish a metallic flavor and gray coloring. Plastic freezer bags make excellent, easy and disposable marinating containers.

Remember that fish absorbs marinades much faster than beef or chicken. Most fish will marinate in 15 to 20 minutes. Fish also may partially cook from the acid in marinades, so be careful about overcooking.

One of the simplest and best tricks for adding flavor and instant zing to any fish is to sprinkle lightly with Lawry's, McCormick or other salt-free garlic-and- herb seasonings. This stuff is great. When it's combined with a rub or marinade it can turn a below average fish dinner into a great meal.

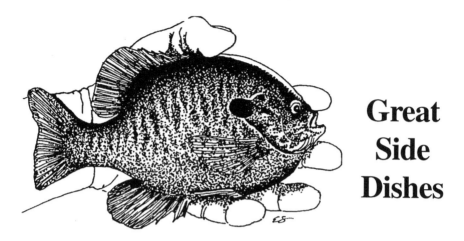

Great
Side
Dishes

Fish is simple food, but the whole focus should be on its natural flavor. That's why I'm an uncomplicated cook who pushes simple recipes. The shorter they are the more unique fish flavors come through. I also want excellent natural flavors in side dishes that compliment the fish. I can usually do that with the crunchy texture and flavors of fresh produce. Here are the best ideas I've come up with.

MUSHROOMS SAUTEED WITH GARLIC

1 pound medium white button mushrooms, quartered lengthwise
1 tablespoon olive oil
2 tablespoons butter
4 small onions, minced
2 cloves garlic, minced
1/4 cup fine white bread crumbs
3 tablespoons chopped parsley or chives, or both

Saute mushrooms in the oil and butter 2 to 3 minutes or until lightly browned. Season with seasonings of choice or salt and pepper.

Add onions, garlic and bread crumbs. Stir and toss until lightly cooked, about 4 to 5 minutes. Add herbs. Serve hot and placed next to fish cooked by any method, Serves 4. This recipe has been used by French fishermen for centuries.

ASPARAGUS WITH TOASTED PARMESAN CHEESE

94

1 pound ultra fresh spring asparagus
2 tablespoons butter, melted
1/4 cup grated Parmesan cheese

Steam or simmer asparagus about 7 minutes or until tender. Drain and arrange half the spears in a buttered shallow baking dish. Drizzle with half melted butter and half of the Parmesan cheese. Cover with remaining asparagus and top with remaining butter and cheese. Place under pre-heated broiler 3 or 4 minutes until the cheese is hot and bubbling. Serves 2. Be sure not to overcook the tender young asparagus.

ASPARAGUS WITH LEMON GLAZE

1 pound ultra fresh spring asparagus
2 tablespoons butter
1/4 cup lemon juice
1 teaspoon Dijon mustard
1/4 cup chopped chives

In a small saucepan melt butter over low heat. Add lemon juice, mustard and 1/2 chives. In large skillet bring two inches of water to boil. Place asparagus into skillet. Cook spears 6 to 7 minutes or until bright green and tender but still firm. Drain in colander and place on warm serving platter. Pour lemon glaze over spears. Garnish with remaining chives. Cut into bite-size pieces. This lemon glaze adds some zip to bland, lean fish, especially those that are poached or braised. Serves 2.

SAUTE OF SQUASH, ONIONS AND PEPPERS

1/4 cup olive oil
1 cup thinly sliced medium onions
1 cup chopped red bell pepper
1 cup 1/4-inch-thick slices small yellow squash
1 cup 1/4-inch-thick slices small zucchini
1 tablespoon minced garlic
1 tablespoon unsalted butter
1/4 teaspoon lemon juice

In a large skillet, heat oil over medium-low heat. Add onions and red pepper. Saute about 4 minutes or until wilted. Add squash, zucchini, garlic, seasonings. Stir to combine. Add lemon juice by drops while stirring squash with wooden spoon. Saute about 8 minutes or until squash softens. Remove skillet from heat, add butter, stir until mixed. Turn into serving bowl. Goes great with fish cooked by any method. Serves 4. Garnish serving plates with orange slices to add even more color.

CORN ON THE GRILL

There's an old adage that you should start boiling the water just before you head out the back door to pick fresh corn. You don't have to pick corn that fresh, but the fresher the better. Here's why. Each passing hour means that any just picked vegetable begins burning its stored natural sugars as fuel for its metabolic processes, thus reducing flavor, texture and nutritional content. The natural sugar content of just-picked corn is at its peak, perfect for developing by grilling with the husks on. This is why this recipe is so special. It's even more special with a couple of small stream trout per person grilled at the same time.

> 2 small trout gutted and scaled, but with heads attached
> butter or margarine
> 4 ears fresh corn on the cob with husks peeled back, silk removed
> 6 sheets heavy-duty aluminum foil (roughly 15 X 8 inches)

Place one trout on one sheet of lightly greased foil. Sprinkle with Lawry's Lemon Pepper or Garlic and Herb Seasoning, wrap loosely and crimp edges to hold in heat. Repeat process with other trout. Place one ear of corn on sheet of foil and sprinkle with lemon pepper and Lawry's Seasoned Salt. Dot with butter and push husk back into place. Loosely wrap and fold aluminum as with trout. Repeat with remaining ears of corn. Grill trout and corn together over medium-high heat for about 10 minutes on each side. Serves 2. (Note: This recipe is from Lawry's booklet titled "Game Recipes." For free copy, plus other recipes, write Lawry's , Dept. MAR-PR, P.O. Box 1088, Grand Rapids, MN 55745-1088.)

A big bowl of tossed salad goes great with simple grilled meals like this. I top my salads with a couple spoonfuls of cottage cheese and a favorite dressing.

ROASTED BABY BEETS AND NEW POTATOES

12 baby beets 2-3 inches in diameter, trimmed and scrubbed
12 new small potatoes, preferably reds, scrubbed
2 tablespoons virgin olive oil
3 whole garlic cloves, peeled, thinly sliced
1/2 cup chopped fresh chives
3 tablespoons unsalted butter

Preheat oven to 400 degrees. Put all vegetables into ovenproof baking dish that will accommodate them without overcrowding. Pour on olive oil. Dot with butter. Season to taste. Bake, occasionally stirring to ensure even cooking for about 45 minutes depending on size of vegetables. Remove from oven and stir in chives. This magnificent dish goes well with any fish. So, while veggies are cooking, saute, deep-fry, broil, grill, poach or braise most any species of fish you happen to catch. Broiling probably is best bet because you already have a heated oven.

FRESH GREEN BEANS WITH PASTA

1 1/2-pounds fresh green beans
4 tablespoons butter or margarine
2 tablespoons lemon juice
olive oil
lemon wedges
1 pound uncooked pasta

Cook beans at a rapid boil for 3 minutes or until just tender. Drain and set aside. Melt butter in small saucepan and stir in lemon juice. Bring pot of water to a boil, drop in pasta and cook to directions. Drain and toss with just enough olive oil to give it light coating. Divide and place onto 4 serving plates. Drizzle with lemon butter. Top with beans and cooked pieces of fish. (Peas or chunked asparagus work as well as beans. Herb butter also is great substitute for lemon butter.)

HERB BUTTER

1 stick unsalted butter at room temperature
1 clove garlic
1/2 lime and 1/2 lemon, pits removed

1/4 cup mixed fresh herbs most any combination to suit taste, (Some of best include parsley, dill, basil, majoram, rosemary.)

Peel and finely chop garlic. Juice enough lime and lemon to measure 2 tablespoons. Wash fresh herbs, pat dry and chop finely. In food processor or blender, combine all ingredients and process until well mixed; or knead same ingredients together by hand in small bowl.

Form herb butter into log-shaped roll about 3 inches long. Refrigerate for several hours or freeze for quick use in 1 hour. Melt for drizzling as in above recipe, or any other use requiring melted butter.

SAUTEED SPINACH WITH ONIONS

2 pounds young spinach
1 medium onion
4 tablespoons unsalted butter or margarine
1 lemon
1/2 orange
seasoning to taste

Wash spinach, remove stems, place wet leaves in medium-size bowl. Peel onion and chop enough to measure 2 tablespoons. Squeeze juice from lemon and orange into small bowl. Remove pits. In large skillet heat butter over medium-high heat. Add onion and saute for 2 minutes. Add spinach and toss to combine with butter and onion.

While spinach is still bright green push to one side of skillet and pour in citrus juices. Then toss everything to mix and cook until spinach is ready to eat, another minute or two. Season to taste. Serve alongside any grilled or broiled fish steaks or fillets.

Some great side dishes are cooked right with the fish. See BROILED WALLEYE FILLETS ON SPINACH BED in chapter 8. Here's another recipe that utilizes fresh vegetables.

BRAISED WALLEYE WITH "MELTED" TOMATOES

4 6-ounce walleye fillets cut in halves
(Substitute any other white-fleshed fish)

2 teaspoons olive oil
3 tablespoons chopped green onion
2 teaspoons minced garlic
2 cups peeled and diced tomatoes
2 tablespoons dry white vermouth
lemon wedges for garnish

This recipe is made to order for an electric frying pan, or large high-sided skillet. Heat oil in pan over low heat. Add onions and garlic. Cook until softened and slightly golden, about 5 minutes. Add vermouth and simmer 1 minute. (To peel tomatoes, place in boiling water about 30 seconds or until skins crack. Plunge into cold water, then pull off skins.) Dice tomatoes and add to pan. Simmer 5 minutes until just warmed through. Add seasonings to taste. Remove everything to a large bowl and set aside.

Put about 1 inch of hot water in pan. Add 1/4 teaspoon salt. Bring to boil. Add pieces of fish. Lower heat to simmer. Braise 8 to 10 minutes. Remove fish with slotted spatula and place 2 pieces in centers of 4 warm serving plates. Cover with "melted" tomatoes.

A variation of above recipe calls for 1 1/2 cups diced tomatoes mixed with 1/2 cup diced yellow bell peppers. This combination adds color and a bit of zip to plain white fish.

You can make great side dishes with raw vegetables, too. Try a design of cherry tomatoes, green or yellow zucchini and white button mushrooms. Begin by paring the zucchini then cutting into thin slices and arranging lengthwise in the center of a round serving dish. Slice the tomatoes in half, then arrange on one side of the zucchini. Slice mushrooms in quarters lengthwise and arrange on other side. Top everything with chopped chives or sprigs of parsley. Baste with salad dressing if you wish. Such ideas are endless.

Atlantic Salmon
And

The Freshness Factor

This chapter is for any man or woman who loves eating fish but can't catch any or has used the last package from the freezer. This may be a temporary situation for those who are too busy to fish often enough. It may be a permanent problem for those who never learned how to fish. The category even includes persons who have no desire to go fishing. All of these people have one common problem ... no fish to cook. The solution is buying fish, a situation that has seen an enormous improvement in recent years; due partly to the Atlantic salmon story. Today, if you know how, you can buy a few species of fish almost as fresh as those you catch.

This is a far cry from the old days. Leo Yeck, a longtime friend who died recently at age 87, worked on commercial fishing boats when he was a young man. This is what he told me:

"You could stand at any commercial fishing dock on the Great Lakes and see baskets of unloaded fish sitting in the sun in the middle of a cloud of flies. The commercial fisherman didn't get any more for quality fish than he did for garbage, so quality didn't matter to him. That kind of attitude went right down the line. The fish market starts out with fish that's days, maybe a week old. They don't want to get stuck with it. If it doesn't sell quick they rinse it in brine every night to keep it from smelling too bad. Later somebody buys it and they wonder why it tastes awful."

That kind of fiasco doesn't happen in the <u>best</u> retail fish markets today. For contrast, take the commercial Atlantic salmon that are farmed in many locations in North America. They follow an express, straight-line path to market. Twelve to 16 hours after being netted from clean salt water, they are in a fish market most any place in the nation, ready for early-morning steaking or filleting. When you buy salmon like that you can cook fish as fresh as if you caught it yourself.

This only happens at the very best outlets, The top choice may well be a combination fish market and white-tablecloth eating establishment. The success of these places depend almost entirely on the availability of fresh fish cooked to perfection.

You can also buy fine quality at supermarkets boasting seafood departments that are separate from meat and poultry sections. These establishments are serious about selling fresh fish because that's the only way they can keep enough customers to justify maintaining a special section.

Then there are the speciality fish markets that copy the very best specialty meat markets selling only the premium cuts of domestic meats. This is ironic because many people assume that farmed fish probably is inferior to wild fish, yet they are well aware that farmed beef, pork, lamb and poultry is the best there is. The reality is that farmed salmon -- thanks to more careful handling and faster shipment to market -- usually is equal to wild salmon.

So there are a lot of plus factors for buying fish when you can't cook your own, but there are plenty of negatives to buying fish from the secondary markets.

In the traditional seafood market freshness and quality is spotty, at best. Even in the mom-and-pop small markets located in the harbors where the commercial boats come in daily, you really don't know if you're buying fresh fish. Be wary of the small retail markets that sell smoked fish in addition to so-called "fresh" fish. Some of this fish that is days old and well into the spoilage stage is smoked to save it from total loss.

That is why I wrote, in the introduction to this book, that there is no way anybody can cook a great fish dinner by using inferior quality fish. And that's what you will likely get from any retail operation (market or restaurant) that uses unfrozen fish from the wholesale level.

Frozen fish is an entirely different story. Most consumers have the idea that "fresh fish" means that it has never been frozen. What fresh should really mean is that the flesh hasn't begun to deteriorate. If fish is frozen properly soon after being caught and cleaned it will stay fresh for months until it is thawed.

This is what happens to quality fish that are harvested by the best commercial fishermen. Even though their boats may be at sea for weeks, their catches are cleaned and flash frozen shortly after being taken from the water. When these fish, still frozen, are delivered to the retail market or restaurant and not thawed until ready for sale or cooking they are of top quality.

Fish of various kinds have been raised in farm ponds in Europe and Asia for centuries. In North America aquaculture is a relatively new phenomenon. Farm-raised catfish is a booming industry in the United States, but the Atlantic salmon industry is the first aquaculture enterprise to reach a worldwide market. It got its start in the mid-1960s when Norwegian researchers began raising salmon in dammed saltwater estuaries.

There are two major reasons for this ever-brighter picture. First, of course, is the booming demand for fresh fish; particularly salmon. According to the U. S. Department of Agriculture, the consumption of fish in America has risen 22 percent in the last 10 years. Of even more importance is the fact that penned salmon can be raised far more efficiently than other farmed meat.

Chickens, for example, convert feed at an efficiency of around 5.5 to 1, meaning that 5.5 pounds of feed are required to produce one pound of edible chicken. Pigs convert feed at a ratio of 7 to 1. Beef cattle register about 15 to 1, while Atlantic salmon comes in at only 1.5 to one.

Research and development efforts in aquaculture have focused on Atlantic salmon because their fillets and steaks are so appealing in both sight and taste. But they also fetch a high price in the marketplace. Catfish is cheaper. This species accounts for over half of all the farmed fish production in the United States. Annual total farmed harvest of catfish is over 350 million pounds, with most of it coming from Mississippi where it has replaced cotton as the states largest industry. That's an enormous amount of fish, a tribute to its taste which is equal to or better than wild catfish. Blind taste tests have repeatedly shown this to be true.

This is not the case with rainbow trout, another important species in the U. S. aquaculture industry. About 60 million pounds of rainbow are produced annually, so there must be plenty of buyers who like to eat farm-raised trout, which in my opinion, can't compare to the great quality of wild trout. Trout farming has been an established business for about 100 years.

No matter what species of fish you buy, the main consideration is freshness. Always remember that most wild fish are cleaned at sea, even though the boat may not dock for a week. Top quality farmed fish get to market in less than a day. Even so, fish freshness is relatively easy to check. Use the following guidelines:

FRESH WHOLE, DRESSED, OR DRAWN FISH

Good Quality

Clear, bright eyes (some fish such as walleye have cloudy eyes)
Bright red gills
Flesh firm, springs back when pressed
Ocean-fresh, slight seaweed odor
Scales tightly adhered to skin
Belly cavity (if gutted) clean, no blood or viscera
*Whole fish has head on. Sometimes gutted and gills removed

Poor Quality

Dull, cloudy, sunken, bloody eyes ·
Brown or grayish gills
Soft, flabby flesh separating from bone
Sour, ammonia-like odor
If scales present, dull or missing areas
Belly cavity (if gutted) with trace of blood or viscera.

FRESH FILLETS AND STEAKS

Good Quality

Bright, consistent coloring, almost translucent
Ocean-fresh, slight seaweed odor
Firm, elastic flesh ,(springs back when pressed)
Clean cut edges, evenly trimmed
Moist but not slimy

Poor Quality

Flesh bruised brown at the edges
Sour, ammonia-like odor
Soft, mushy flesh
Tears, ragged edges
Dry or slimy

FROZEN FISH

Good Quality

Flesh is solidly frozen
When thawed, pass same criteria as fresh
Tight, moisture-proof package
Product visible, unmarred

Poor Quality

Flesh is partially thawed
Signs of drying out, such as paper edges
Packaging is torn, crushed on edges
Shows signs of ice crystals or freezer burn

If you can't examine the fish up close, there are still ways to determine the freshness factor.

1. Look for properly iced displays. It should be crushed ice and there should be enough ice to keep the fish cooled to 32 degrees Fahrenheit.

2. No cross-contamination ... no smoked or otherwise cooked fish touching raw.

3. Properly displayed identification and price markers that don't touch the fish.

4. Ask your retailer how long he has had the fish and where it came from. It's bad news if he doesn't know or seem to care. It's good news if he knows exactly how fresh it is, and he tells you he is going to take some home for his family's dinner.

5. Watch what other shoppers are buying, then ask one or two about the usual seafood quality in the store.

While good quality can be purchased, it's still a poor substitute for fish you catch yourself. There's a certain magic to catching wild fish and bringing them home for dinner. Years ago I was on a crappie fishing trip in Kentucky. Hope Carlton, a DNR public relations officer, and I were cooking fish one evening when Hope looked at me and said: "The three most important things in life are a good woman, homegrown tomatoes and fresh crappie fillets!"

You can feel that way because not only do you get the best fish in the world to eat, you also get the satisfaction of belonging to a very select group of individuals who take great pleasure in many ways from successful fishing trips. There's a sense of celebration in eating fish that we catch, and knowing that there are a lot more in the freezer. It's gourmet subsistence because just having wild fish to eat proves the presence of special knowledge, skill and persistence. It's a great deal more satisfying than buying fish for several reasons. For one thing it's likely that the fish you're going to have for dinner can't be purchased in any commercial market.

Take those crappies fillets that Hope Carlton and I were frying in Kentucky. You can't buy crappies in any store. If you want those golden brown fillets on your plate you have to catch them. The same is usually true for many species of fish, including, smallmouth and largemouth bass, brook and brown trout, northern pike, and some species of ocean fish.

You're in elite company when you tell your stories of how you caught the fish you're serving for dinner, because sometimes you can't catch any no matter how hard you try. I have a buddy in Florida who owns a 1/4-interest in a 18-foot backwater fishing boat. One evening last winter Jim and his co-owners were downing a few beers at a big party. The conversation turned to eating fish. With all the confidence of men who have caught thousands of fish, Jim and his cohorts invited everybody at the party to a big fish bake the following Friday. The only problem was that they had to catch the fish they were going to cook.

Best Fish Ever

"That trip turned into one of the worst flops of my entire fishing career," Jim told me later: "Everything went wrong. The cold front put the snappers off their bite, so we went after trout in a back bay where we always get 'em. Not a bite all day. The next day was even worst because we could hardly hold the boat steady enough to cast into near hurricane winds. We caught absolutely nothing in two days. It can't get any worse than that."

Every angler runs into fishless days. There's no guarantee in this sport, but you can have bonanza trips of action too. Some days fish seem to hit your bait no matter where you cast it.

Jim and his buddies had planned to bake snapper or sea trout because 2-to- 5 pounders of these species are ideal for baking whole, thereby saving the time of filleting a large number of smaller fish for the crowd.

Baking works great because the even heat crisps the outside while cooking the interior relatively slowly. This process helps avoid overcooking any part of the fish.

Bake at high heat, 400 to 425 degrees in a preheated oven. Jim claims that his baked fish is best when stuffed with a few herbs and aromatic vegetables. He begins by spraying baking pans with no-stick cooking spray. The pans are arranged on an oven rack. The fish are placed on the pans and seasoned on the top sides, then cooked in middle of the oven.

Small whole fish in the 2-pound class will bake perfectly in 25 minutes. Larger fish will take up to 45 minutes. Fish fillets or steaks will bake in 15 to 20 minutes. A 2-pound whole fish will make 3 servings. Two pounds of fillets will serve 4.

How To Freeze Fish

Well-frozen fish has good color, texture, and flavor. When fish is frozen quickly, the ice crystals that form are tiny. Later, when it is properly thawed, those tiny ice crystals melt inside the flesh. When this happens the fish is nearly as moist and full of flavor as it was when it was first cleaned and frozen.

The opposite of this situation occurs with the freezing of far too many sport-caught fish. Problems usually develop when the fish is frozen too slowly in freezers that aren't cold enough. When this happens, larger ice crystals are formed that are capable of rupturing cell walls in the flesh. When such fish is defrosted, two problems arise. The larger ice crystals contain too much liquid to be reabsorbed into the flesh, and additional liquid is lost from the broken cells.

The lost liquid is termed "drip loss". It affects the weight of your fillets, plus a corresponding loss of flavor and texture because flavor elements are part of the cells original liquids. They drip out right along with the moist qualities of the original flesh. The result of all this is dry, and far less tasty fillets or steaks.

Drip loss is most often a problem with fish frozen by inadequate equipment. All the older model frost-free refrigerators have freezer compartments that don't get cold enough. The newer models that have freezer-compartment temperature controls will work fine if you can get the temperature down to zero degrees. That's the ideal temperature for freezing fish.

Best Fish Ever

The best way to ensure top-quality freezing of fish and game is to own a good quality upright freezer. Chest freezers are cheaper to operate, but it's considerably more difficult to locate specific packages in them. Never under buy in size. Figure that the average family needs four cubic feet of frozen food per person. If you have four hearty eaters in your family you'll want at least a 16-cubic foot unit.

By all means buy manual defrost models. The cost of running one is considerably less than frost-free models, but of most importance is the fact that frost-free models are notorious for drawing moisture out of frozen fish. This is especially true of the freezer compartments in frost-free refrigerators. You simply can't get top quality frozen fish unless you use an all-freezer unit that maintains constant temperatures close to zero degrees.

Drip loss problems also result from faulty wrapping and faulty defrosting. Always remember that air is the major culprit in stealing flavor from your fish. The secret is to eliminate all air from the meat. There's no way you can do this by wrapping your fillets in freezer paper or foil because you can't possibly eliminate all the small air pockets. Wrapping in a couple of layers of freezer-type plastic wrap is better, but it still doesn't do the complete job of freezing in an all-covering layer of ice. Ice is the only airtight and air-free covering you can use.

Why is this so important? Because freezer burn—the dehydration of meat, especially fish— can occur very rapidly in the ultra-dry air of modern freezers. This is why most authorities on freezers say that wrapped and frozen lean fish should be used within four months, and that two months is the limit for oily species. Personally, I have far better luck than that with fish frozen in water, especially lean fish. On occasion I have found walleye, pike and panfish packages in my freezer that were two years old. When I finally cooked those fillets they were just as good as the day I froze them.

Oily species are a different story because their fat can begin turning rancid within weeks no matter how they're frozen. I have a couple of friends who fish almost exclusively for salmon. They cut their fish into steaks and grill them a couple of times each week. When the fishing gets really hot they freeze the few fish they don't release. By October, when

108

the salmon runs are over, they remove the frozen packages from their freezers, defrost the fish and can them. This way the meat will last for years instead of rapidly losing quality.

Herewith is my formula for properly freezing fish.

Step 1: If the fish eventually will be fried, poached, braised or grilled, it should be cut into serving-size pieces. This reduces the amount of water needed. The less water used the quicker the defrosting is accomplished, and the less the fish flesh is softened by water.

Step 2: Select the size zip-locking freezer bags you should use. A pint bag will hold enough fillet pieces to serve two persons, a quart bag up to four. Mark each bag with the species of fish, freezing date and the number of servings the bag holds. Use a felt-tip marker. If I cook a big dinner I can use several bags totaling any desired number of servings.

Step 3: Put the pieces of fish into the bags just large enough to hold the pieces plus water to cover. While holding the bag upright in a sink, fill with cold tap water. Slosh the pieces around in the bag to eliminate any bubbles.

Step 4: Begin closing the bag by moving thumb and forefinger along the seal. As water continues flowing from the bag's top finish zipping until the bag is completely closed. If done correctly you have an air-free bag because it contains nothing but 100 percent fish pieces and water. There is no way this packaged fish can become freezer burned as long as the bag doesn't rip or become opened, and it remains at about zero degrees.

Step 5: After freezing, most of the fish pieces are separated by ice so little sticking together occurs. This makes defrosting easier and quicker. Defrost in a bowl in the refrigerator or under cold, running water. If using water, put the fish in a colander so draining occurs as soon as the ice melts. Dry with paper toweling before batter dipping, flouring, or other precooking preparations.

It's best to schedule your off-season fish-cooking sessions by species in your freezer. The oiler the fish the sooner it should be cooked, especially the larger and older specimens. The worst offenders are lake trout. Many laker fishermen won't keep a laker over 5 pounds. Many others will eat lakers the same day they're caught, but won't freeze them. Salmon, steelhead and whitefish aren't as bad, but they still have short-term freezer life.

The leaner species, such as pike, walleye, smallmouth bass and panfish will freeze and stay in prime shape for many months, probably years. The same is true for the bland saltwater species including snook, sea trout, groupers, porgies and flounder; all of which are highly esteemed table fare.

If you buy fish, there's a way to tell which fillets or steaks will freeze the best. The lighter the color of the meat, the lower the fat content. Pick out fillets that are almost white. They'll always have less fat than the oiler and darker steaks.

There's one last way you can freeze fish if you have the time and patience to do the work. It's the highly effective technique of glazing. Commercial processors use it to save space and diminish water loss. You can mimic the process at home. Here's how it's done.

Step 1: On a tray or baking sheet, place rinsed pieces of fish in a single layer with space between them. Set the tray in your freezer for an hour or two.

Step 2: Remove tray from freezer. Dip the pieces one at a time into a bowl of ice water. The water will form a thin layer of ice all over each piece of fish. Rearrange glazed pieces back on the tray and return to freezer.

Step 3: Repeat the glazing process every half hour until you have three or four coatings of ice on each piece of fish. Pack all pieces tightly in plastic freezer bags and store in the freezer.

This technique saves freezer space because you don't use as much water, but it's also less efficient for the same reason.

Still another way to freeze fish is to vacuum-pack the pieces . Manufacturers of the machines claim the vacuum-packed bags of fish will maintain just-caught freshness for up to two years if properly frozen. Get details from Tilia, Inc., 800-777-5452.

How Changing Conditions

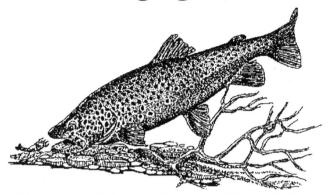

Can Affect Your Cooking

An old guide once told me, "You can't cook 'em if you can't catch 'em! And you can't catch 'em if you don't fish where the fish are!"

These days it's very possible that you're not fishing where the fish are because they're gone, fished out by too many meat-hungry anglers who put too much pressure on a fragile resource. In many cases that cause is far too much commercial fishing, but sport fishermen can wreck an area too. A very dramatic example of this happened to me practically in my front yard. The whole unfortunate mess was my fault.

Back in 1980, when I'd already been Midwest Field Editor for Outdoor Life for 15 years, I wrote a feature for the May issue titled, "Fill-Your-Freezer Time Is Now". Here is part of what I wrote:

> During the first two hours of fishing Dick and I boated about 30 bluegills. We spread them out on my filleting table and filleted them all, then went back out fishing. We went through four sessions of fishing and filleting that day. For 12 hours all we did was catch fish and clean them.

Today, no editor in his right mind would allow such selfish writing to appear in his magazine. But back then readers wanted that kind of reporting. They wanted to know where they could go to catch as many fish as possible. And I told them. I told about two million readers where they could catch enough bluegills to fill their freezers.

I still live on the shoreline of that lake in Northern Michigan, and I fish it about 100 times a year. The panfish populations that once numbered hundreds of thousands still haven't returned to normal. So if you believe great fishing waters can't be fished out you would be wise to change you mind. It happens all the time, especially these days when modern electronics make catching fish so much easier.

In 1998 the National Marine Fisheries Service (NMFS) acknowledged that at least 86 major fish stocks are severely depleted. The Service reported that the situation for Chinook and coho salmon in the Pacific Northwest; king mackerel and red snapper in the Gulf of Mexico; and many other species throughout North America are tiny fractions of their former abundance.

Great programs are now being initiated to restore declining fish populations. One example is the recent sudden increase in catches of pompano by anglers on the west coast of Florida. It all coincides with the commercial net ban that took effect a couple of years ago.

Texas' Lake Fork has become one of the state's hottest largemouth bass fisheries, thanks to an intensive slot-limit program that's consistently producing bass over 8 pounds. While slot limits aren't the answer for more fish in all waters, new regulations imposing different limit structures have dramatically improved fish populations in many appropriately selected waters.

Fish managers are continually fine-tuning new rules to satisfy different groups of anglers. For example, slot limits that produce more trophy fish often have the counterproductive catch-and-release of too many smaller fish. Since any given acre of water can produce only so many total pounds of fish, some waters can become overpopulated with small fish. In this case managers may increase the limits to entice the hook-and-cook group to take home more small fish. This actually helps to produce more trophy fish, so everybody is a winner.

In other cases fish managers are removing minimum size limits in waters where there are too many small fish of a given species. Next spring I'm going to fish a lake that has become overpopulated with small northern pike. The size limit of 24-inches is dropping to 20 inches. And believe me, a 20-inch pike makes great eating.

Ponds and small lakes are being targeted for panfish management in many states. Biologists develop shallow bedding areas and other structure for optimum fish reproduction and growth. When these waters become established a small fee is charged for daily or annual use. It's a far different story on what used to be some of the best fishing waters in America.

The belief that the vast West has a large supply of wild trout that seldom see a fisherman may be the biggest myth left in the realm of fishing. To begin with, much of the West's finest trout areas are owned by very wealthy people or by ranchers. There is either no access or limited access that goes for big bucks. The river sections open for public use are becoming a joke. A fishing buddy of mine just returned from Montana. "I probably saw as many guided river boats as pickup trucks," he told me.

A cheaper way to catch fish for dinner is to join a fishing club. Privatization has already proved its worth where clubs own or lease their lakes or streams. Angling clubs with exclusive rights to particular waters use management techniques that provide much higher quality fishing than is found on nearby public waters.

Many states are also easing overfishing pressure by creating fish management areas. Biologists improve fishing in these areas by getting rid of nuisance aquatic plants, stocking new species, installing fish feeders, and doing whatever else is necessary to take pressure off existing popular waters. All of this creates thousands of acres of improved fishing waters.

Another way of spreading the angling pressure is lowering catch limits. A few years ago many states had no bag limits on panfish, a sure route to overfishing during spawning periods when mature fish are concentrated. Going from a no-limit to a 50-fish-per-day limit, then further reducing it to 25 fish daily has been a very successful procedure. Biologists agree that this approach distributes the catch of adult panfish. Restricting the catch through proven management techniques produces recoveries in many species of fish.

Increasing the numbers of catchable fish is also taking some modern twists that were unheard of in the old days. Biologists are now using a new trick for producing big bluegills in a hurry. They have discovered that when they net stunted bluegills from an over-populated lake, then plant them in a reclaimed lake with ideal habitat, the tiny fish will grow from a few ounces to nearly a pound in less than a year. It would take a newly-hatched 'gill at least four years to reach that size in average waters. Fish managers are still trying to figure why this happens, but they know for sure they can produce a lot more big bluegills.

Cutting down on flagrant poaching is another way to supply you with more fish. Virginia Marine Resources Commission officers attempted to seize a gill net from two men fishing illegally. They soon found that the net was far too long and heavy to move by hand. They radioed for a dump truck from the state's highway department. Even the truck had a hard job pulling that net on shore.

"Those guys were arrogant to the end," said one of the officers. "They joked they didn't care about the fine because they'd made $8,500 the second day they used the net."

Modern law-enforcement practices are cutting down on such outrageous violations. It's just one more technique of supplying more fish for the sport angler.

Another bright spot is the growing realization among anglers that they have an enormous potential for political clout. According to the U. S. Fish and Wildlife Service, 35.2 million people in America participated in fishing in 1996. The National Sporting Goods Association claims that fishing participation outstrips golfing by 2 to 1. If organized politically, anglers could carry any election Federal or state, pass any legislation in their interest, and get fisheries management decisions into the hands of trained biologists.

In the past, commercial interests have been able to influence management issues to their benefit. Now, anglers are beginning to realize that the key element in all management decisions should be having healthy fisheries. Winning this issue will also mean future growth for sport fishing.

Perhaps the final answer to getting fish to cook is in lowering our expectations. If we don't adjust to resource realities we're sure to miss out on a lot of the fun. Certainly fishing won't be as good as it once was for some species, but it may be better for others. We have to go for what's available, and not lament for what used to be. If the bluegill populations are way down in a lake where you use to get them, maybe the walleye bite is up in another lake not far away. It's up to us to find the action.

Lowering your catch expectations won't make you a less capable fisherman. If anything, it will make fishing more enjoyable because you'll have a better outlook on why you go fishing. The single-minded goal of filling your freezer with fish has been replaced with more anticipation for simply enjoying the sport. You'll keep angling tied to its authentic food-gathering roots, but you'll pay little attention to trying to catch your limit. Boating enough for a meal can indeed make for a successful day. So can releasing everything you catch.

Fishing has become so big time that it's now mainstream. The February 16, 1999 issue of USA TODAY devoted its front page Cover Story entirely to modern angling. It's headline read "Fishing Has No Boundaries. It can be something for everyone."

The story claims there are now 29.7 million freshwater anglers plus 9.4 million who prefer saltwater. It proves that recreational fishing is booming.

Why is this? Because fishing is one of the few opportunities left to enjoy a wholesome sport in the great outdoors. Just being there gets us into a beautiful place to be. Fishing enables us to spend quality time with family and friends while casting away the rat race.

USA TODAY claims the average angler goes fishing 17 days each year. That helps explain why 58 percent of today's anglers practice some form of catch-and-release fishing. Any angler with experience can't possibly eat all the fish he'll catch in 17 days. He wants to put something back into his sport, so he releases fish for others to catch.

This sharing of the bounty has helped make fishing a huge business. If it were a corporation, recreational fishing would rank 13th among the Fortune 500 list of America's largest businesses.

Fish Soups, Chowders, Stews, Smoking, Canning and Pickling

One of today's major themes promoted by professional cooking writers is "Cook Now, Eat Later." The idea is to cook in large quantities when you have the time, freeze in meal-size containers, then parcel the meals out when you're pressed for serving dinner in a hurry.

This quick fix has become so popular that several books have been published on this single subject. Some of the best include "Frozen Assets: How To Cook For A Day And Eat For A Month," "Dinner In The Freezer," and "Once A Month Cooking."

The bad news is that most of these tricks won't work with fish. As a general rule leftover fish, even when eaten the next day without freezing, has lost at least 50 percent of its quality. Leftover fish that's frozen becomes almost unpalatable. Fish is at it's absolute best when it's cooked shortly after being caught, and at its absolute worst after being cooked, frozen and rewarmed at a later date.

Smoking, canning and pickling are the only excellent ways to prepare fresh fish for later eating. I'll get to these procedures in a moment, but first I want to talk about fish soups, chowders and stews. These dishes, made with fresh fish, can be delicious and have just about everything going for them. Nutritionally, almost nothing is wasted. They're easy to prepare, abundant in flavor and beautiful to look at.

A major key for success is choosing fish that are at least moderately firm. (See chart on page 62.) Such fish won't fall apart in simmering liquid. And steer clear of oily fish because fish oils can give soup too strong a flavor. That happens because these cooking methods hold in fatty juices.

Fish broth (stock) is a major component. It can definitely be frozen in advance because it contains no solids. Fish broth needs only 20 minutes of cooking, but don't add salt when you make it. If you add salt now you'll lose later control of how much was used. Preparation includes saving and freezing fish-bone sections (heads and organ tissue removed) every time you fillet fish. Make a big batch of broth and freeze it in both pint and quart containers so you'll have on hand the amount that each recipe requires.

My batch contains about 3 pounds of fish bones, 2 cups chopped onion, one cup sliced celery, 1/2 teaspoon dried thyme, 2 whole cloves of garlic and 8 cups of water. Place all ingredients in pot, bring mixture to a boil, skim off foam and simmer for 20 minutes. Let broth cool in the pot, pour through a fine-meshed strainer and freeze. I generally make fish soup with one simple recipe. Early fall is best because I get fresh vegetables from the garden.

    4 cups lean fish cut into 1-inch pieces
    10 cups fish broth
    1/2 cup chopped onion
    2 cups peeled and chopped tomatoes
    1/4 cup chopped fresh parsley
    2 cups chopped green bell peppers
    1/4 teaspoon cayenne pepper
    or other seasoning to taste
    2 cloves garlic, crushed (optional)

Put everything except the fish into medium-size pot and bring to a boil. Lower heat and simmer for 20 minutes. Add fish and bring back to a boil. Lower heat again and let simmer (covered) for 10 minutes. Serves 6 to 8. Croutons are optional.

Chowders are little more than thick soups usually without tomatoes but with several other ingredients added. If you have accumulated some assorted pieces of lean fish, chowders are the place to use them. The following ingredients make 8 servings.

3 tablespoons butter
1/4 pound good bacon fried, drained and crumbled
2 large onions, chopped
6 medium potatoes, peeled and cut into 1/2-inch cubes
8 cups fish broth
3 pounds boneless lean fish, cut into 1/2-inch chunks
4 cups milk
1/2 cup flour
1/2 teaspoon dried thyme
1 cup chopped celery

Put potatoes, onions, celery, thyme, butter and seasonings to taste into pot with broth. Bring to a boil. Reduce heat to simmer about 10 minutes or until vegetables are tender.

In 1-quart jar with tight-fitting lid, combine flour and milk. Shake until smooth. Gradually stir into vegetable mixture and cook over medium heat for 5 minutes or until beginning to thicken while stirring frequently. Add fish and cook for 10 more minutes. DO NOT BOIL. Garnish each serving with crumbled bacon and chopped, fresh parsley.

Fish stew is a thicker dish than chowder, but doesn't include milk, flour or bacon. To the other ingredients add:

6 carrots, halved lengthwise, cut into 1/4-inch slices
6 small zucchinis, cut crosswise into 1/2-inch slices
3 cups fresh or frozen peas
3 average size bell peppers, diced
1/2 teaspoon red pepper flakes
3 cloves garlic, chopped
5 tomatoes, cut into 3/4-inch pieces, use juice to reduce fish broth quantity to 6 cups

Put all vegetables and broth into pot or large skillet. Bring to boil, reduce heat and simmer 20 minutes or until vegetables are tender. Stir frequently. Add more broth if needed to prevent stew from getting too dry. Gently stir in fish pieces. Simmer 6 to 8 minutes or until fish is just done. Serve hot with seasoned bread and tossed salad. Some folks prefer serving this stew over bed of pasta.

Smoking is one of the best techniques for cooking oily fish, especially today with the many quality smokers on the market. When I learned the art many years ago we used an old refrigerator for our smoker. And our brine solutions were complicated recipes that took hours to prepare. The drying process was also tedious. Most of that stuff is history today because modern equipment allows almost instant smoking. You can buy a combination smoker/cooker that's also a smoker/grill, a deep fryer, a fish poacher or a camp stove. See Cabella's or Bass Pro catalogs, or check K-Mart and Wal Mart.

We do most of our smoking by using the Dry Method in a kettle type charcoal grill. Start the coals on one side of the rack. In a gas grill heat the burners on one side. Put presoaked wood chips (apple, cherry and other fruit woods are great for smoking fish) on the coals in a perforated foil packet or metal smoker box. It's important to soak the chips for at least half an hour because the wood will burn and not smoke if it's too dry.

Place the fillets on the grate as far from the fire as possible. Close the cover and position the open top vent over the cooking area. Regulate the heat with the bottom vents, opening a notch to increase the temperature and shutting to decrease it. Dry smoking requires a low cooking temperature, 150 to 200 degrees. Thin fillets may smoke in little more than an hour. Whole fish may require several hours.

Even if you don't have an outdoor grill you can try the stove-top method to see if you like your fish smoked. Put a half inch of presoaked chips in the bottom of a roasting pan. Elevate a wire rack about 2 inches above the chips with balls of aluminum foil. Place fillets or pieces of fish on rack and cover the pan. Heat the pan on high until the chips begin to smoke. Lower the heat to medium and smoke the fish until it's done.

Luhr-Jensen makes an inexpensive electric smoker that keeps a constant, ideal temperature without tending. It costs about $45. A similar unit made by Brinkman goes for about $30. Their top-of-line electric smoker (about $100) also grills, steams and roasts. Easy to follow directions (and some recipes) come with most of these units. They make today's smoking of fish easy and very popular.

Rubs or marinades add delightful flavors to smoked fish. Check chapter 10 for details.

Canning salmon may be the best way of cooking fish now and eating it later.

> Filleted and skinned salmon cut into 1 1/2-inch pieces
> 1 teaspoon Kosher salt per pint jar
> 2 tablespoons vinegar per pint jar
> pint jars, lids and rings for quantity to be canned

Pack salmon pieces snugly to within 1 inch of top of jars. Add salt and vinegar. Wipe jar mouth clean and seal with hot lids and rings that have been simmered. Screw down tight. Place jars in pressure cooker set at 10 pounds of pressure. Cook for 90 minutes.

While canned salmon is delicious, pickled pike has been a gourmet treat in my family since almost forever. Pike is the only fish we pickle, because we make it from the Y-bone strips of meat and bones that are residue from filleting. (See sketch on page 49.) Other species of lean fish are also great for pickling.

For a gallon of pickled fish make a broth of:

> 8 cups white vinegar
> 4 cups sugar
> 2-1/2 cups Kosher salt
> 4 cloves garlic

Simmer until sugar and salt is dissolved. Let broth cool while cutting pike strips into bite-size pieces. Submerge fish in broth and add 8 tablespoons pickling spice. Refrigerate 5 days, stirring each day to ensure total mixture. Remove fish pieces, place in colander and rinse several times under cold water. Let stand 45 minutes while cutting 6 medium-size onion into slices.

Pack layers of fish and onions into 4 one-quart jars, beginning with layer of onions on bottom of each jar. Leave 1-inch head space. Cover with pickling broth and 1 clove garlic. Cap and store in refrigerator 4 weeks before eating. Bones disintegrate.